MISSPENT-MY LIFE IN RETAIL

MISSPENT-MY LIFE IN RETAIL

JULIE NISCHAN

This book is dedicated to:

In memory of my dad, thanks for the work ethic

To my mom, who taught me to get back up and try again tomorrow

I'd like to thank my husband for his total support and encouragement.

Thank you to all my friends I have made over the years working in retail. I could not hope to find any more true and honest friends anywhere.

Big thanks to my editor Joel Pierson

<u>**Cover art by Derith Trickey**</u>

-

1

Retrospection comes easier as you get older. You see that the years ahead are fewer than the years behind, and you start thinking about where those years went and how you used them. We spend so much of our lives working; we call it trying to make a living. But aren't we living while we are working? If not, then has it all been a waste? As I look back over a thirty-year career, I find myself searching for meaning while trying to convince myself it has not all been for nothing.

Of course, how do you measure what is a waste? Compared to some, I'm sure my time would seem to be wasted. To others, I have had a blessed and fruitful job filled with joy and achievements, life lessons, and amazing friends. The only one I can measure to is myself and my own expectations of what I wanted it to be.

When I was little and was asked what I wanted to be when I grew up, I remember I said I wanted to be a pilot. I loved heights and thought it would be great to fly a plane so high up in the sky. But I was told I could not do that, as I wore glasses, and you had to have perfect vision to be a pilot. How could you fly a plane if your glasses got broken? (I think my mom just told me that because she didn't want me to be a pilot.) I don't know if that was true, but my hopes of being a pilot were dashed. I also announced that I wanted to be a bus driver or work at McDonald's. (One had just opened in the small town nearest our farm.)

My mom wanted me to be a teacher like her, and I'm sure wanted me to aim higher than fast food. I didn't care that much for school and had no intention on continuing to go to school my whole life!

It's easy to have big dreams when you are young; I certainly had my share. As a small child, I wanted to be famous enough to be invited on *The Muppet Show*. I had no idea what I was to be famous for, I just knew famous people got to be on *The Muppet Show*, and I wanted to be on the show, too. I also wanted to be a writer, or a singer, an actress, or musician, or a racecar driver. But my family is a very practical lot, with my mom being a teacher and my dad a farmer; so, our dreams didn't go much higher than "get some education, get a decent job, and have a family."

I always wanted to be the best at something. Whether it was sports or music, or just to be the smartest in the room for once and save the day somehow. I am the youngest and most average of my family. Where my siblings excelled at school, band, and music or sports; I was just middle of the pack, not the worst but certainly not the best. I have learned many things, but I have always been the "jack of all trades, master of none." We were also taught to think for ourselves; don't just stand around and be told what to do. I was always taught that you can be part of the pack, but you don't have to follow it.

I guess I shouldn't feel too bad about being average; most of us are, whether we know it or not. Though it certainly is easy now to gain your fifteen minutes of fame on the internet. When you have no talents to speak of, just be as ridiculous as possible, and that will probably do. I never watch YouTube videos; watching some fool who can make more in a month than I do in a year just for being stupid and having others record it is just far too depressing. I see plenty of stupid each day and have never felt like someone should be paid for it. I'm old school and feel that you should actually have a talent of some kind to be famous.

But not having a true talent leaves me here, and some days feeling very stuck. Stuck in a job not that's not really a career; stuck in lower to middle class unable to rise above; stuck daydreaming of a big break that will never happen, no matter how many unlikely scenarios I imagine.

I started in retail not knowing where it might lead, and I certainly didn't anticipate staying so long. If you can make it a year, it seems like only a minute later you realize it's been five years, and you can't believe it's gone so fast. The joke is when you hit ten years, you are considered a lifer; twenty years, and you are institutionalized. Thirty years is dead, leaving a soulless husk stalking the aisles. So, when I hit twenty-nine years, I could literally hear the clock start ticking.

Now I find myself reflecting on how I got here and all those I met along the way. Retail has been my working world for the last twenty-nine years. As I plan retirement, I think back and wonder two things: how in the world did this happen, and what do I have to show for it besides two broken feet and a lot of gray hair?

The problem is that after too much time at any job, you can no longer afford to quit. You make too much in pay and benefits to leave and start over at the bottom of the ladder. I can't start over at minimum wage with no insurance, no vacation days, and no 401(k). But I have overstayed my welcome. It used to be a good thing to stay at one job; it showed reliability and pride in your work and company. Now it seems to look like you are inflexible and unable to learn anything new, or too scared to try. When you have spent all your time in retail, other companies assume you were a cashier or stocked shelves and don't give you a second look. It's very hard to get them to realize that along the way, you have learned many skills valuable to any company. Problem solving, being able to work unsupervised, and the ability to learn new skills are things that every company needs from its workforce. And I know how to fix almost anything, because I've seen almost everything done incorrectly. (You never say you have seen it all; someone will always take that as a challenge.)

2

My dad believed three basic things about work: that no matter your job you should do it to the best of your ability; there are no days off in farming; and chores wait for no man. I had never wanted to go to college, but just getting a job and living at home was not an option. I grew up on a farm in north central Kansas, and jobs in our nearby small town were limited. My parents had worked very hard so their children could get a higher education and better themselves. My siblings were at the top of their classes and received merit scholarships to help pay their way. I, as the B-average student, did not. Knowing higher education would never be for me, I started college knowing I would never finish. I started because it was expected of me. I had no desire but knew I must leave the house and start being an adult or never hear the end of it.

So, I went and figured I would see what happened and figure out my future as I went along. I started classes and soon found that before I could take anything that actually interested me, I would have to enroll in many subjects that did not. This seemed to me a huge waste of my time and money, the latter of which was running short already. I spent three semesters going to class on and off before officially quitting. I was working part time on and off campus anyway.

I met a young man and started dating. I didn't plan to get serious, but he had other ideas and proposed to me after two weeks. I didn't want to get married right away but didn't want to brush him off completely, so I said yes and thought I would end it later if things started to go awry. But I didn't end it, and we grew closer and started making long-term plans. We were married eighteen months later. We felt we had waited long enough to appease both sets of parents, but now I look back and know we were very young. We were both twenty, and he turned twenty-one ten days after our wedding.

We talked about starting a family. I thought a couple of kids; he announced he wanted at least six. I told him he would have to give birth to half of them, because I had no intention of having that many babies! We decided that since we were both very young, we would just wait and see; we would start a family when the Good Lord decided we should. I had no strong urge to have children, so I was content to wait and see if I got pregnant or not.

As for our marriage, let me just say that opposites attract but are a huge pain in the ass to live with. We are about as opposite as it gets, so fights, arguments, and hurt feelings have been constant companions to us. We do love each other very much. I certainly know he loves me all the time he is driving me nuts, and I try to make sure he knows I love him too, even when I want to kill him. Most of our marriage has felt like a tug of war against each other, but we were both taught that you don't give up on something just because it's hard; you just work a little harder. That and the Good Lord have kept us together all this time.

We talked recently about whether we would have done things differently so long ago when we were both briefly attending college. I said I wish I would have gone to a trade school of some kind, wished that possibility had been presented to me. He agreed but did point out that if I had gone to a trade school, we would never have met. I can hardly fathom how different my life would likely be if we had not met. But I meant from a working/career standpoint, I wish I had learned a skilled trade and would be making a better living and feel like I was actually accomplishing something, not just plodding through the daily grind.

Work is easy to find in a college town; every food and retail shop needs help, and turnover is high, so businesses are always hiring. I had worked since I was sixteen at a retirement home in the small town near our farm and worked on campus in one of the food services. So, heading into full-time work didn't scare me. I checked around some places and found the large retail business in town with the best starting pay, so I put in an application and got hired on. I was average at book smarts but knew I had street smarts and a good dose of common sense. This gives me three talents in the workforce; I learn quickly hands on, I can problem solve, and I make decisions on my own. All three of these get scarcer at work every year.

Retail is like waiting tables. Almost everyone has done it for a while, but only the really good or really crazy stay. Believe me, I have never met anyone who started and planned to stay forever. Most plan to work six months to a year until they find something better. But as time flies when you are having fun, it can also fly as you are trying to pay the bills. It's hard work on your feet for little recognition and even less appreciation. If you have never worked retail, you have certainly shopped at a retail store. If you've never thought about the jobs there, consider this: 99 percent of the employees work on their feet all day, either standing in one spot cashiering or walking around the store stocking shelves or building displays and such. Most who work the floor average five miles of walking a day on concrete floors.

It's physically tough but mentally tough too. The to-do list never ends, plus you have customers to help, co-workers who call in, and God help you if corporate comes to visit! Then the whole place is in a panic, desperate to make it look like perfection is achieved daily. You spend days putting lipstick on the pig, just to have the bigwigs walk the store for ten minutes before retreating to an office to discuss sales and wage goals and then breaking for a two-hour lunch. Then they head back to the main office, and you get back to work, back to the regular madness. Mostly you spend your days trying to put everything in the back room out on the sales floor, basically stuffing fifty pounds of shit in a five-pound bag. My days shoveling manure on the farm prepared me well.

A retail store has three main zones. First is the front end, which includes the cash registers, accounting office, and return desk. This is the front line, with the most customer interactions. Next is the sales floor, the heart of the battle. All who work the floor hear the same comments daily. "Can you help me?" "Do you have any more in the back?" "I've been wandering around for fifteen minutes and haven't seen a soul. Doesn't anyone work here?" "Why are you always out of everything I want?" "Where the hell is the pet section? Every time I come here it's in a different spot!" And of course, my favorite is: "This place sucks! I'm never shopping here again!" Once when I was feeling particularly sassy, I replied back, "Thank you for shopping. We'll see you tomorrow!" (The customer was not as amused as I was.) Last is the back room. This is where the battle scarred go to lick their wounds, dry some tears, and re-caffeinate before heading back into the fray.

I've worked in all three zones in my years, and each has its pros and cons. Sometimes you never leave your zone, and other days you run between the three your whole shift. No matter what company, store, or job you have in retail, there are some universal truths:

- Plans change at a moment's notice.
- Expect the unexpected.
- You will make friends and enemies.
- You're selling toilet paper, not curing cancer. It's really not that serious.
- The place can and will run without you.
- No matter how bad your day was, try again tomorrow.

3

Over the years, I have worked at three different locations with thousands of different people. I remember the best and the worst, both times and people. I guess that's how memory is; there is only so much room for storage, so the extremes stand out, and the rest becomes a blur. Feelings become attached to the extremes, locking them in, and most times these events start to mold and change who we are.

I can remember my first day in retail when I was just 19 years old. Not specifics, just that there were twelve of us filling out paperwork and learning about dress code, rules, and schedules. By the time six months had passed, only two of us remained; by the end of a year, I was the only one left. That's not surprising, most who start leave within a year.

I can and will talk to most anyone, so interacting with customers and coworkers was never a problem. Keeping my opinions to myself, though, that took me some time to learn. I remember one of my first bosses telling me she didn't care how much I talked, as long as my hands were as busy as my mouth! I took that to heart and learned to multitask constantly. It's a skill not everyone has, and I see many who stop completely every time they voice a thought. No wonder they don't get anything done. I'm used to carrying on conversations while working, no matter what I am doing. When much of your work is repetitive, it is not too hard to learn to split your focus.

The first area I worked in was the snack bar. Most stores don't have them anymore, but they used to be very common. We sold popcorn and soft drinks, hot dogs and chips, and even baked cookies in a tiny oven. And of course, coffee was our staple. Many customers would come get a cup, and almost all the employees would fill their mugs for break time. We had a small seating area of booths, and six of us prepped the food, rang up orders, and cleaned the whole area throughout the day. There were a group of six old men who came every morning to chew the fat and drain the coffeepot. They stayed a few hours, and we all got to know each other quite well. I liked them; they reminded me of the old farmers my dad would talk and drink coffee with at the grain elevator most mornings. Before I was old enough to go to school, he would take me. While the farmers discussed politics, wheat prices, and livestock, I would wander down the hall to the secretaries to beg some candy.

The women I worked with were a good group. We were all about the same age, except our lead, who was closer to my mom's age. She was a nice boss who taught us to be friendly, clean often, and keep that line moving. I enjoyed the work and quickly memorized the price of each item and could quote our bestsellers with tax. (Medium popcorn, seventy-eight cents.) About a year after I started, the store had a complete remodel, and we were sent to be cashiers while the snack bar was closed and rebuilt. I didn't like it as well. Customers usually stopped by the snack bar on their way in and were happy to get a snack to enjoy while they shopped. At the registers, the lines never seemed to end, and by the time most customers reached me, they were impatient to leave and often not very pleasant.

When the remodel was finished, our new snack bar was unveiled. It was lovely. Twice the size with brand-new everything. A self-serve pop machine, double coffeepot setup, and a shiny new popcorn popper. The morning of the store's grand reopening, it was all hands on deck. The store manager and visitors from home office were to have a ceremony at the front doors, while the employees waited for the customers to be allowed in to see all the changes. My boss and I were to open the new snack bar for the first time. When we came in to make sure everything was ready, we discovered that someone had been concerned about flies in the store and had put out those hanging fly strips. But they didn't hang them; instead they laid them across many of the tables. We pulled them off and missed the entire opening ceremony, trying to remove the sticky residue off our brand-new booths. Not the opening we were hoping for. I scrubbed furiously while a line started to form, and as soon as I cleaned the last table, I ran to help my boss with the large crowd. Crisis averted.

I was satisfied with the job, but a strange thing happened at my first performance review. A manager took me into an office and addressed me in a very serious tone. "If you don't start changing your work around here, you'll be fired in a week," she told me.

I was shocked. "Why? What on earth have I done wrong?"

She glared at me. "You come in late. You stand around and talk instead of working. And last week, you were seen in the break room for forty minutes. What were you doing?"

I could feel my temper rising but fought to hold it back. "If I was in the break room for forty minutes, then I'm sure I was taking my lunch break. What day was it? I can get my timecard, and we can look at it now. I do not come in late, either. I try to be five minutes early, so I can get any notes from those leaving for the day. Let me get my timecard, and I'll show you." I stood up, and she got angry.

"I don't like your attitude. You need to be respectful to me," she growled.

I glared right back at her. "I don't appreciate people who lie to my face and try to intimidate me." We stared each other down for a minute.

Finally she spoke. "Well, these are things one of the other managers told me."

"Maybe they have confused me with someone else," I said, matching her even tone.

"I'll look into it. Go on back to work."

I nodded and left the room. I never heard another word from her about being fired, but I definitely watched my back around her.

Even though I had not worked there a long time, I had no intention of being intimidated by someone who was lying to me, whether they had the power to fire me or not. I believe very strongly that no person is better than anyone else, just because you may have more money or power than another. It usually just means you can buy nicer things, not that you are smarter, more important, or somehow "worth" more than me. I kept my distance from that manager and became good friends with my boss and coworkers in the snack bar. We were a small group who worked well together and supported each other. I was sad to say good-bye when my husband and I chose to move to a larger city with more opportunities.

We moved about an hour away for a fresh start. My husband started a new job, and I transferred to a different store within the same company. A bigger city meant a bigger store, more than double the size and number of employees. I started in the deli and did my best to learn quickly and fit in. One of my new coworkers was Roxie, a motherly woman twice my age. She was a hoot to work with, as she would start six tasks while never finishing one. I often came behind her and finished what she had started. She didn't so this on purpose; she was just easily distracted. She would help herself to small "samples" of the meat, cheeses, and salads we sold by the pound. She insisted that we must try each product so we could tell the customers about the taste and quality of what we were selling. I taste-tested almost everything in the display cases but drew the line at head cheese and souse. (The description of it was literally head cheese with pickles. No thank you!) I liked my new area, and just as I was going to learn some of the supervisor tasks, I had an accident at work and had to have surgery on my knee, so I was put on light duty. I had to be able to sit most of the day, so I went to help in one of the offices.

The woman I worked with was a real character. Everyone in the store knew Ruby; some loved her, some hated her. I liked her immediately. She was loud and funny and always spoke her mind. My first day with her, she pulled my chair close and leaned toward me.

"I'm going to tell you the most important thing you can learn in retail. Forget the company's core principles. This is the true golden rule."

I sat forward and listened intently. She cleared her throat dramatically. "It is easier to ask forgiveness than permission," she declared, and then cackled with laughter. Although I didn't know it at the time, she was right. These were indeed words to live by.

She challenged every supervisor; most didn't dare fight with her. Ruby was a good teacher, not just showing you how to do something but also explaining why. I learned a ton from her, about different jobs in the store and how to deal with all kinds of coworkers. She butted heads with one woman in particular; they were as opposite as could be and never saw eye to eye. Once she told me how the other woman asked her to come to a quiet office with a third coworker so they could pray for a troubled employee. Halfway through, she realized the woman being prayed for was herself! Ruby just went along and thanked the two for their prayers when they were done. She laughed and laughed when she told me. I don't know if I could have handled it so well! Now that I'm a lot older and a little wiser, I think I could, but not back then.

She taught me a lot about problem solving and figuring things out on your own. She was never afraid to make a mistake. She told me everything is fixable; you just have to know who can fix it if you can't. We did a lot of troubleshooting for the store together, learning the ins and outs of the computer system and how to find mistakes and fix them quickly. Ruby also wrote guidebooks for different major retail events. Her Black Friday guidebook was still used four years after she retired.

4

After eight months with Ruby, I was asked to move from her office in the back to the front of the store and work in the cash office, counting and processing all monies for the store. So, I switched offices and started to learn something new again. I was nervous to move to the cash office, as math had always been my weakest subject. There were eight of us who worked in the office, which had to be staffed the whole time the store was open. A number of girls came and went while I was there. A couple were there before me and still there when I left. One of those was a real piece of work. I called her "Blondie" for her dyed blonde hair. She and I got on like oil and water. I had girls who were vindictive and back-stabbed me before, but nothing like this. I had never seen someone work so hard to make another person so miserable. I didn't hate her first off, she was just another coworker. But she felt she was the queen of the office and should be treated as such.

She wasn't the supervisor but bullied that woman into getting her way daily. I saw no reason to treat her specially; she was just a coworker doing the same tasks as me. And when I started to do the tasks better than her, she started to be very nasty. She would make up gossip about others and claim she heard it from me. Blondie would hide other people's things and insist I had moved them. I wasn't worried; as long as I showed up for my shifts and got my work done properly, there wasn't much that could be said. At least she didn't spend too much time in the office. She left the room constantly to walk around the store and spread gossip and shop with her friends. We all knew that's what she was doing, but since the supervisor was scared of her, nothing was done. The rest of us just enjoyed the peace while she was gone.

I also worked nights, so I only saw her for an hour a day as our shifts overlapped. Once she had left for the day, the mood became lighthearted in the office. The evening girls working with me were fun; we often laughed so loud that a supervisor would come to tell us to quiet down. Customers could hear us. I met my best friend working in that office, and Vee and I quickly became like sisters. We have been friends for over twenty years, and we still tell stories from those days. I don't know if I could have dealt with the Blondie without Vee having my back.

The cashiers loved to play jokes on us. There was a small room behind the customer service counter where we would interact with the cashiers. We could speak and hand them money bags through a window between that room and our office. They would come to the window and receive cash for their till to start their shift and bring it back at their lunchbreak or the end of their shift. (A till is the tray the money sits in that can be removed from the register drawer.) Cashiers picked up a moneybag from us with a preset amount in it and laid it out in the till to start their day. As they waited on customers, the tray would fill and then be emptied back into the bag and the bag handed back to us. We spent most of our shifts counting and logging the cash, checks, and credit card slips from each till. Everything had to be double counted and entered into the computer. The program tracked every cent incoming, and we would prepare deposits that would be picked up by armored car and taken to the bank.

At shift change, the cashier room would be quite full as bags were picked up and dropped off. Some cashiers would leave little candies in the moneybag; others preferred rubber spiders or bugs for us to find. One young man stuffed a rubber snake in his bag and caused quite a panic. One of the women screamed hysterically and pushed another down as she ran out of the room. Vee helped her up as I collected the snake and removed it from the office. A manager brought our terrified coworker back in and tried to calm the situation. Both women insisted they needed to go home, one to lie down and one to ice her bruises where she had landed on the floor. The manager finally let them leave, and Vee and I were left to finish the work. At least we had each other!

Working with Vee, the days were easier, even the double shifts we worked because coworkers called in. I was grateful that she had been raised with a strong work ethic, as I had. We would be scheduled off, but too often, the next shift person would call in, and one or both of us would stay and work, so the third-shift woman didn't get shafted. We were always there for each other; we'd come in on days off to help the other get the work done. Plus, we had a lot of fun. Vee was such a klutz, she didn't have to try hard to get everyone laughing. We had office chairs that you could adjust the height, and once she dropped a pencil under the counter and tried to reach it without getting out of the chair. I kicked the height lever, and she got stuck under the counter, unable to move the chair and wedged in completely. I had a good laugh at her helpless situation but did finally get her out. She and I helped each other through some tough times. She helped keep me sane at work when Blondie had me ready to quit. We have been best friends for years, and I still tell everyone she is my little sister.

I worked in the cash office with Vee, Blondie, and others for four years. I continued to learn new things; ten-key, new computer programs, and research and correction skills. I wasn't sure how well I would do in accounting; math was always my worst subject in school. I am good at very basic math, which was really all I had to use. I learn new things by doing them repeatedly until I become comfortable with it. I became the fastest in the group at ten-key, but I found that easy since I did it most of my shift. Eight hours a day, forty hours a week, fifty-two weeks a year is a lot of practice. Everything had to be double counted—cash, checks, credit card slips, even coupons. And every check had to be encoded for the bank. This was just before debit cards, so it was common to spend an hour or two each night encoding the day's checks, which meant more ten-key. This also meant the start of carpal tunnel. The oldest member of the team, who had worked in the office for many years, helped me. She had both wrists operated on for carpal tunnel and advised me to get a wrist brace and wear it all the time. I had to learn how to type and ten-key wearing the brace, but I never had to see a doctor for my wrists. That twelve-dollar brace saved me thousands in medical bills.

I loved to work with my girl, Vee. She could always be counted on to be entertaining. She loved to sing and would just randomly break into song whenever the mood struck her. She'd suddenly announce that it was way too quiet in the office; this was the cue that a concert was about to start. Unfortunately, she sang the same songs over and over again. I didn't mind "Henry the Eighth" and could even put up with "The Song That Never Ends," but "The Old Lady Who Swallowed the Fly" drove me nuts. And once she got started, there was no stopping. She'd sing that damn song through every stinking animal till the old bitch finally swallowed the horse and died, and we'd all say it was about damn time too!

Vee was quite blunt; we used to joke about her lack of tact when talking to others. That's just how she was raised, to be truthful and to the point. I tried to teach her that you catch more flies with honey than with vinegar, but she often spoke before she thought about how her words may come across. Good thing I have a thick skin and don't get offended easily, or our friendship may not have lasted. One day we were all comparing our driver's license photos. I swear whoever takes them used to do mug shots. Mine is always terrible, but since the other girls passed theirs around, I did too. After a good laugh, I said that I thought mine was better when I had short hair. Right after I got married, I had it cut quite short and kept it that way for a few years. Vee wanted to see a picture of me with short hair, so the next day I brought one in to show her. She took a long look and announced that she liked the longer hair better; the short hair made my face look very fat. Half the room laughed; the other half scolded her for being rude. She apologized; she hadn't thought she was rude, just truthful. I just laughed and hugged her and told her it was a good thing I didn't have feelings, or they would really be hurt. I wasn't upset by it; I prefer a tough friend who tells you the truth, no matter how painful.

Another time, my mom had made me a new shirt for my birthday. My mom was a great seamstress and had often made our clothes growing up. She even sewed my bridesmaid dress I wore for my sister's wedding. She could make shirts or dresses so well, people swore they were store bought, not homemade. So, the day after my birthday, I came to work in my new shirt, very pleased with it. It was button-up blouse style, in cotton fabric. The pattern was all cartoon like cats in bright colors, yellows, oranges, and greens. I was quite proud and showed it off and told everyone how my mom had sewed it for me. The other girls couldn't believe it; they checked the back for a store tag. I got a number of compliments until Vee showed up for her shift. Before I could even say anything, she took one look and asked loudly where I had gotten that bright ugly shirt. Everyone gasped, sure I was going to let her have it. I rather sharply informed her that it was a gift for my birthday, made by my mom, and that I happened to love it. She quickly decided that it wasn't that ugly, just the colors were too bright for her taste, and my mom had indeed done a lovely job sewing it. We did laugh about it later, and I wore it every year for my birthday, just to poke at Vee.

Another skill I developed in the cash office was forgery. That sounds terrible, but sometimes you have to forge a manager's name on reports just to keep the work moving. Of course, I had a bit of experience back in school forging my dad's name on permission slips. His was easy—just put pen to paper and sneeze. I still can't copy my mom's; as a long-time teacher, she has that beautiful, flowery handwriting that is murder to try to copy. A manager was to sign off on the reports every day, as it was something that was checked when we had a quarterly compliance visit. But getting someone to take ten minutes of their day was too much to ask, and the reports would pile up. More than once I was told to just sign them myself, so I started practicing and could copy most of the managers' signatures well enough to fool the others, sometimes even themselves. It's been a useful skill over the years; I always get a sample and practice as needed with different managers. They sign so many things that they never remember anyway. Besides I've had so many managers tell me to just sign reports, work orders, delivery slips, and the like that I don't even ask anymore. I just sign and go on. On the grand scale, no one will really notice, and no one cares anyway.

Many new programs were added to the company computer system—electronic schedules, record retention, and how the monies were tracked from the registers changed. Almost everything was moving from paper to computer or handheld scanner. Many of the girls in the office and the cashiers were unhappy about the changes. I have never been one to be afraid of change; I think most optimistic people handle it well. I try to be pretty optimistic, despite my complaining when things go wrong! I always try to think of every outcome to a change. It could be a disaster, it could be great, but it's almost always somewhere in the middle. If the situation you are in is terrible, what's the worst that could happen in a change? You could be just as miserable, or you could be much happier. I for one am always willing to try the change.

When the supervisor left, a new one came in for about a year. I liked her a lot; she was friendly and fair and saw through the bullshit of Blondie. She was a lot of fun and enjoyed joking with all of us about Blondie. One office task was boxing old reports to be taken to the storage graveyard in the attic of the store. It was a creepy place; only a few of the lights worked and the AC compressors were so loud that someone could sneak up on you with a running chain saw, and you would never hear it. I was about the only one brave enough to take boxes up to the attic. I would box most of the reports, but another woman decided she wanted to do that job. I hardly cared; there was plenty of work to be done. Reports would be boxed and labeled with the contents and a destroy date. This woman was very careful to neatly pack the boxes and label in large print DESTORY with the correct date. It was pointed out to her more than once that she had not spelled *destroy* correctly, but she just went about her business, either convinced we were wrong or just teasing her. She did it on every box, even when I would complete a box and set it on the counter next to her, she would still write DESTORY every time. We just all shook our heads at it and figured no harm done.

She did cause harm once though, and our new supervisor almost lost her mind over it. The store had gone through a remodel, and we were allowed to paint the interior of the office our choice of color. We all voted on a cheerful light green, hoping it would keep morale up more than the depressing beige. The next morning after we had painted, the supervisor and I came in to find that this woman had decided to label keys kept by the door herself. A few sets of often-used keys were hung by the door so they could be given out easily, keys for the cash registers and manager's office and the toilet paper and such in the bathrooms. The supervisor had planned to make neatly printed labels to hang above each set, but this woman had beaten us to it. The supervisor looked horrified to find that she had written on the fresh paint with a Sharpie marker! The worst was her sloppy scrawl of reg (for register), man office (managers office), and for the bathroom, she had written TAMPOON in large letters. While the supervisor turned three shades of red and tried to scrub the marker off, I stood back and laughed till I cried. One of the male managers came in to see what was going on, stood dumbfounded, and asked what the hell a "tampoon" key was. I told him it was for when you were having a really heavy period and were bleeding like a whale. He got very embarrassed and left the room; we didn't see him cross the doorway for a month.

When the supervisor left, Blondie and I both applied for the supervisor job. Blondie assumed she was going to get it since she had seniority over me. But the manager of the front end (running all the cashiers, office employees, and supervisors) had plainly seen what Blondie was doing, (i.e., not working), so I was chosen to be the new supervisor.

Soon after I took over, I was called to a meeting with other supervisors to discuss a new training manual for that area. The others waxed poetic about how much they relied on the current manual, referring to it daily. Then I was called on to share my thoughts. "What I need is the troubleshooting chapter expanded. I know what to do when the sun is shining and everything is rosy. I need to know what to do when a tornado has touched down and rabid wolves are chasing people through the store." They all just stared at me like I wasn't even speaking English.

"I don't understand what you mean," said the woman in charge.

I opened the book and showed her what I meant. "All this has is the number for the store support hotline. Every time I have called, they put me on hold for twenty minutes, then log my question and give me a reference number. If you're lucky, you will get a call back twenty-four hours later. And if you are really lucky, they might even have solution for you. Known fixes to common problems would be helpful." The whole room just looked at me blankly and continued on about new chapter headings and such. When I received the new manual about six months later, the troubleshooting chapter had been removed completely, and the store support number was printed inside the back cover. So, I wrote my own chapter and added it to the book, detailing how to fix unusual problems that I had encountered. It's something I have done in most areas I have worked, creating a book of answers to problems or common questions. Now when coworkers call me at home, I just refer them to the big book. The answer is probably in there somewhere.

Everyone else in the office was happy about my promotion over Blondie. They certainly knew she would make everyone's life miserable if she were in charge. Instead, she only set out to make mine miserable for "stealing" her job. She worked very hard at it and had obviously had a lot of practice. I was not raised to treat others badly; my first-grade teacher used to tell us, "If you can't say something nice, don't say anything at all." So, I tried to stay quiet around Blondie, refusing to sink to her level. Most people would tell me to fight fire with fire. But I've learned that it only makes me look bad in the end. Plus, if anyone said something rude or mean to her, she would run to file a complaint against them. I never really got in trouble from her complaints; it was just another thing to annoy me. One of her favorite tricks was anytime I was on the phone; she would come close to me and make rude and snotty comments just loud enough for me to hear. She knew I couldn't say anything to her while I was on the phone with someone else. When I hung up, she would move away and go back to work. If I addressed it then, others in the room would look surprised; none of them had heard her say anything. She did it all the time because she knew it irritated me.

Every time we had an office review, she took her chance. If I was off that day, or every time I was out of the office, she would hide reports, move documents, and be sure to tell any story she could think up about me. I had already put up with her for three years as a coworker and one year as her supervisor.

Vee transferred out of state to care for her grandmother, and my best friend and best ally was gone. The others in the office liked me, but no one was going to stand up to Blondie for me and risk being in her line of fire. Plus, there were a number of new faces in the office that caused a lot of bickering between the other girls. I was tired of it and becoming completely stressed out, so I asked to move out of the office. I had put up with enough and decided that I would rather change areas than continue to be miserable coming to work every day. I spoke to the store manager and told him I didn't care where I was moved; I just insisted on a move. I would rather push carts in the lot than continue working with all the drama.

5

The store manager decided that there was an area he needed someone to clean up, and I was moved to the claims department in the opposite end of the store. I hoped distance from Blondie would lower my stress levels. I rarely saw her after that, but the woman I worked with was one of her best friends. So now I had a new problem coworker, but at least I only had one, not a roomful. This woman, Patsy, had an instant hatred for me, partly because of Blondie and partly because I am white. I enjoyed the work; it was new things to learn again and always something different to take care of. Things were fine as long as I didn't mind being called a racist every day. Mostly I just let it go in one ear and out the other. The manager saw the good work I was doing and knew I was making the area look much better. He was on my side and begged me to ignore her and keep working in the area; he could not reprimand her because she constantly tried to file complaints of racism. He knew that any complaints she made against me were bogus, and he never addressed any with me. I also got outstanding performance reviews the whole time I worked with her.

I remember one day she was on a big tirade about how all white people in American had owned slaves. She told me my ancestors had, and

I had no right to deny it. I informed her that my ancestors were Irish, and we didn't own anything! It didn't stop her; she just became angrier. I just went back to work and stopped listening. The best time working there was when she was out for eight weeks on medical leave. It was so peaceful and stress free.

I learned a lot there; there were always problems to solve and crazy messes to deal with. Claims is the great dumping ground of the store; any broken or unusual items were dropped off for me to take care of. Almost every item that customers return to the store is brought to claims. Sometimes there is nothing wrong with it, and it gets put back on the sales floor. But most times it is truly broken, and I would scan it out of the system and prep it to ship out. Any item that gets broken or damaged on the sales floor also comes to claims. I always said that the claims employees are the maids of the store; messes are dropped off and left for us to clean up. Broken candles, used makeup, ripped-open packages, and anything dirty or gross. I would have to find the UPC code, scan it with the handheld computer, and choose what was wrong with it. The program would then direct me in the proper disposal. Company dress code doesn't really apply to claims, as it's just a given that you are going to ruin all your clothes. I was allowed to wear jeans and any old T-shirt I wanted as I processed leaking bottles of bleach and spilled paint. If there is a way to clean up a spilled gallon of paint without getting it all over, I never found it.

Once someone from the sporting goods department brought me a small bottle with no lid. "Be careful. You really don't want to get that on you," he told me. I grabbed my scanner and quickly processed the item.

"What is it?" I asked him, trying to keep my distance.

"Doe in Heat. It's doe urine. Hunters use it to attract bucks in deer season."

I got one of the self-sealing bags we used for hazardous chemicals, and he dropped it inside. I got a whiff of it as I sealed the bag. "Wow, that is nasty. But thank you for not just leaving it on the desk and walking away. If I had spilled that on myself, my day would have been over." We laughed as I took the bag to the store compactor and sent it down the chute. It was nice of him to make sure I processed it without getting it on me. Most employees are not so courteous.

Claims is the land of "dump and run." I swear people would hide and watch for their chance to drop an item off while my back was turned. One of the problems I dealt with constantly was items with no UPC code. I must have that code so I can scan the item out of the system. Every item that is sold has a code, but it's amazing how many things make it back to claims without one. Employees would bring me a damaged item. "Here, I found this. Management said to bring it to claims." They would start to leave, and I would stop them.

"Hold on. There is no UPC code. I need that UPC number to process this." The usual answer to this was a shrug. I'd try again. "I can't do anything with this without the UPC code. I scan the code, process the item and it gets taken out of the inventory. But the starting point is the code. I need you to find the UPC code; then you can bring it back to me."

This is met with a blank stare. "I don't know the code. How am I supposed to find that for you?"

"You can go to the floor and bring me one of these that has its code. That would solve the problem." Another blank stare. "Take this back to the floor and find the UPC code for the item. Then you can bring it back. and I will process it." I cannot count the number of times I had this conversation. The employee would leave reluctantly with the item, continuing to give me a blank stare. The end result was always the same. Later I would find the item, usually hidden in some mess I hadn't gotten to yet. And it still had no UPC code. The item had been dumped when my back was turned or when I took a bathroom break. It was a daily occurrence.

Claims is also where any stolen packages are brought. I would have to scan the UPC code on the package in a special screen that only people working in claims have access to. This would account for the loss of the item. I was amazed at the things people would steal, basically everything. Clothing, DVDs, makeup, (lots of makeup), and trading card packages would be dropped off. The top two items stolen? Condoms and pregnancy tests. (Insert your own joke here.) Theft is a big problem where I live; it's well known that people will steal anything that's not nailed down. Give them a minute and they'll take that too. As the years have passed, I've seen customers become more and more brazen. Once upon a time, they would be careful not to be seen. But they no longer care, knowing that employees have no power to stop them. All we can do is report it and watch the thief walk away. I once had a woman ditch her package from the eyeliner she stole just twelve inches from me, and she walked away without a care. Most thieves try to justify it by claiming it doesn't really hurt a big corporation. You may think employees wouldn't care, but we do. Any bonus offered by the home office is tied to how much product is lost to theft. So, when things are stolen, it literally takes money out of the pockets of every employee in the building. And since most live paycheck to paycheck, it hurts us way more than it hurts the entire company.

Again, my problem-solving skills were honed as I taught myself how to research items with no UPC code, how to repack items to be sold, or how to disassemble items for shipping. If I was really stuck, I would call another store and ask for advice, but mostly I just taught myself through trial and error. Claims is a very specialized area, using screens and programs that others don't have access to. This means that when you are short-handed, you won't get any help, since anyone management might send back can't use the programs you do. At best, all a helper could do is help sort through the carts and tubs of merchandise to process and box things for shipping. Most times, it's just easier to do it yourself, and I have never minded working alone.

The day Patsy came back from leave, she immediately started yelling at me. She went on a tirade, telling me she knew I was trying to get her fired and steal her job. I stood and listened to her berate me for about twenty minutes, so angry I was shaking. I had put up with her constant abuse for three years and was done. I went to the manager and said I wouldn't put up with it any longer. I asked to be moved to a different area; I had taken enough of her bull. A new team was being formed to work around the store, helping any area in need, and I was told to join that group, again supervised by my friend Ruby.

6

It was a good group, a good mix of people. Most worked hard. Ruby screened everyone on her team, and if they proved to be lazy or unreliable, they didn't last long with her. My favorite on the team was a man I called Mickey. I joked he was my work husband, since we spent most days working together. He was really quiet and the hardest worker I ever met. He loved to help any woman, always wanting to rescue a damsel in distress, but he was a gentleman about it. He always had to prove he could do any job; all it took to get him to do something that seemed impossible was to tell him he couldn't do it. Mickey immediately would jump up and get it done. Once during a remodel of the store, we were to move pallets of floor tiles from the receiving bay in the back of the building all the way to the front where they were to be installed. Two of us would move the pallets; one would pull while the other pushed. They weighed a ton, so even with two people, it took all our strength to move the pallets. I told Mickey to wait. I was helping with another pallet and would come back to help him; he was not to try to move it alone. Mickey took that as a challenge and started pulling the pallet by himself, and then just to show me up, made it to the front before we did. I scolded him and told him he would hurt himself, but he insisted he was fine. He did accept my help with the last pallet, deciding not to move one alone again.

The team got any tough assignment, like reset an entire area (such as home goods or toys) in just a week. It's doable with seven or eight people; everyone can take an aisle and get it done. But often Mickey and I would work with just one other person overnights. The rest of the team would stay on the day shift and keep helping the rest of the store. We would have to remove all old and discontinued merchandise, clean all shelves, and replace any worn shelves or hooks, put out all the new price labels, and refill the shelves with the new stock. We always came through and got it done, which of course was why we got all the hardest jobs. Just like working with Vee, Mickey and I would stay late to finish any project. We both hated leaving a job undone. Ruby was a master problem solver and taught me a lot about how to do resets without making a total mess of the area and how to display the old clearance items to sell quickly. Some people would just pile the items in carts and push them in the back room instead of trying to get them sold. I never understood that; you had to deal with the items eventually; you might as well do it now rather than later.

One year at back-to-school time, we were called in to try to clean up a bad situation. I don't remember how it got so bad, but the season was getting short, and there was still a ton of product in the back room needing to be put out and sold. So, Ruby asked Mickey and me to do a few overnight shifts and blitz it out. We came in to find two semi-trailers full of merchandise. A full trailer holds twenty-four pallets of stock, so we had forty-eight pallets needing to be sorted, unboxed, and stocked to the shelves. Mickey went to the sales floor and cleaned and made space while Ruby and I sorted and unboxed binders, notebooks, folders, etc. We stacked things on rolling carts, and Mickey took two carts out at a time, pushing one in front of him while pulling one behind. He was very fast and kept up with us very well. Small items like glue sticks and scissors came in square cardboard display boxes, making them easy to just set and go. We just kept pounding it out. I would pull pallets off the trucks, Ruby would unbox and stack, I would clean up cardboard, and

Mickey would empty carts and bring them back while we filled up more for him. We had started at 10 p.m. and planned to leave about 7 a.m. as the day shift came in. We were finishing cleaning up cardboard and empty pallets when Ruby did a count and announced that the three of us had emptied thirty-one pallets of freight in one shift. We considered that a world record (unofficially) and defied anyone to beat it. We did the rest of the pallets the next night and finished stocking the back-to-school area. Ruby was quite proud and boasted of her all-stars when we were back on the day shift. It was quite a lesson in how teamwork and organization can make an impossible task doable.

We matched our record another year working in toys before Christmas. Ruby would have the whole team work overnights for two weeks before Christmas, just blitzing out every single toy in the back room to the sales floor. The team would be divided; usually I would be on the unboxing and pricing team, while Ruby and Mickey would take charge of the stocking and display team. Mickey would build all large displays; he was a master at it. So, anytime we had a large amount of the same toy, he would find a spot and make a display of it to maximize sales. Ruby would have the rest stocking shelves. We weren't trying to be exact; just put dolls on the doll aisle and trucks and cars together so things made sense. Someone would have the job of cleaning up all the cardboard and trash so the rest could all keep working. The crew emptied thirty-one pallets in one shift; everyone was very proud till Mickey pointed out that just three of us had done it, so ten certainly should be able to match it! I enjoyed working on the team. I had good hours and good people to work with and I was able to work all over the store and learn about each area.

With all of our knowledge and experience, Ruby encouraged us to apply for any promotions, like running our own area (department) of the store. Mickey and I often applied for the same areas, but retail is like high school in many ways, and often the most popular get picked first, even if they have less skill or know-how. Many who applied just wanted the pay raise; they had no intention of doing the work required. Mickey was passed over a few times before an area came open that needed his talents.

No one envied him his area. He took over home goods, and it was a real mess. The woman who had just left the area was very lazy. She wouldn't take the time or effort to look in the back room for any items; she just ordered another for the sales floor, expecting the overnight shift to fill it when it came to the store. As a result, Mickey had about five semi-trailers full of merchandise to start working through when he took over in late October. Luckily, Christmas season is big for home goods, and he got permission to stuff the sales floor with anything he found in the back. Needless to say, he got very creative, and there were displays of home goods all throughout the store. He busted his butt and was almost run ragged flushing out the back room. By January, he had the inventory to a manageable level, and the area was running smoothly. I knew Ruby hated to lose him from the team, but at least she knew we would never have to bail his area out!

7

Retail goes in cycles, and not just around the seasons or holidays of the year. Time will pass with no areas open, then one person will leave their area, and it starts a ripple effect. This person will want to move because they are sick of their area; that person wants to change because they are failing and about to get fired. Suddenly, many areas will be open, and many can get promoted at once. I was finally promoted after applying nine times. My first area was school supplies, normally a small area except during back-to-school time. I had a great worker in the area, an older little woman I jokingly called Super Cee. She worked circles around kids a third her age. With her by my side, the freight moved smoothly from the back room to the floor. After back-to-school season was over, the rest of the year was very quiet, and before long, I was getting bored. I was asked to take over paper goods and chemicals too. All three areas were next to each other, so it wasn't too hard to keep an eye on all three. Paper and chem are easy; it's just busywork to keep the toilet paper and laundry soap full all the time. They are always in season; you just have to keep the shelves clean and full and let the customers shop.

As time went on, and I had already worked a number of years in retail, I thought I would like to go into management. My home situation was right—my husband and I had no children to uproot, and he wanted to change jobs anyway. So, to promote and be asked to transfer to another location, even to another state, would be okay with us. I went to one of the managers and asked how I would sign up to be trained to be a manager like him. He was a few years younger than me, with a college degree but much less experience in retail. He laughed at me when I asked him, telling me, "You could never do what I do; you have no education or business training." I was embarrassed and angry and felt completely disrespected. How dare this fool think he was better than me! Just because he had a business degree didn't make him smarter or more valuable than me in day-to-day operations. I had learned much in my years so far and felt my experience should count for plenty. I was angry about it for some time and watched any managers closely, listening to their comments and complaints about their jobs to judge if I had really missed out or not. Most of what I had heard convinced me that I was missing out on a lot of headaches. Eventually my anger passed, and I just kept on working.

A year or so later, the company did a big expansion. New managers were needed, so the standards were changed. Now you could have a college degree or more than two years' retail experience to apply. But my home situation had changed; we had a house, and my husband had gotten a new, steady job doing computer work. It was a good job with steady hours, benefits, and yearly raises. I had gotten raises too and was involved with church activities and friends. We had more solid roots now, and moving was not in the picture.

Most of the managers had moved to different locations. Our store was big and was considered a training store, so new faces came and went every few months. Most who came to train had a very superior attitude; they were going to be managers, and we were just peons. The attitude lasted until they needed help or had questions and had to come to us to be taught how to build displays, understand the computer system, or just learn the jargon we used daily. When one of those new fish was told to "switch out a four-way" and they had no idea what that meant, they learned this pond was a lot bigger than they thought. One young man was different; he was very humble and eager to learn and do well, not just learn how to delegate every job to someone else. He came to Mickey and me a lot and asked questions about what our job was, how did we prioritize our day, and how we managed our time to get things done. I tried to teach him all I could from all the areas I had worked in; I always like to teach someone who is eager to learn. One day he asked Mickey and me if we were going to sign up for the training program. We both told him no. Mickey didn't want to boss others; he just liked running his own area his way and being the best at it. When I told him my story of how I was laughed at, he was shocked that I would have been treated that way. I told him that the time had passed, and I was no longer interested. He kept at us, trying to convince us that it would be a good move for each of us and the company. So, I asked him what his starting salary was. He told us, and now it was my turn to laugh. I told him that I made more than that now; why would I take a pay cut for more hours and ten times the stress? He couldn't argue that, so he stopped asking. He still came to us for guidance till he left for whatever store he had been assigned to. I don't regret my decision; as an hourly employee you have more power to say no than as a salaried manager. When my shift is done, I cannot be required to stay. Nor can I be told I must come in early or skip lunch. I can choose to do those things to help out if I want, but I cannot be made to or disciplined for not doing them. As a salaried manager, you can be moved to another store across town or out of state if needed. As an hourly employee, you can be asked, but not ordered to move.

8

Another area came open, and I moved to the bedding area. I liked it; it was larger than paper and chem, but again I thought it was pretty easy to run. The only thing I needed was a reliable helper. I asked the manager about moving Super Cee, but he said no. She was disappointed, but I had a plan. I love to bake and often make treats for coworkers. I found out that the manager had a sweet tooth and made him some peanut butter fudge.

"That fudge is delicious," he said with a big smile. "I ate the whole container you gave me."

I smiled sweetly at him. "I'm so glad you liked it. It's a very easy recipe."

"Would you make some more for me?" He asked eagerly. I stopped smiling.

"When you move Super Cee to my area."

He looked uncomfortable. "It's not that easy. I can't just shift people every day. It takes time." I had expected this answer and was ready.

"Well, you'll never taste peanut butter fudge till Super Cee is working with me again."

"That's not very fair," he said, looking at the floor.

"Seems fair to me. As soon as you move her to this area, I will make you a double batch. The ball is in your court, buddy." I went back to work and waited. Two weeks later, Super Cee joined me in the bedding department, and the manager came by.

"Here she is. I got her moved to your area." He looked at me expectantly. I started laughing.

"You held up your end of the bargain, and I will hold up mine. I'll bring you some fudge tomorrow." I have always found that food is a great motivator.

I loved Super Cee; she was very dependable and would do any tasks I gave her with a smile. She loved to stay busy, so I would walk the sales floor and see what was needed, then go to the back room and mark boxes with a large X so she would know what to grab and stock when she came in. The only thing she wouldn't do was computer work; she never got the hang of using the handheld scanner for anything but looking up a price and making labels. As she was older, she needed to use a shopping cart to transport items around the area to stock. She couldn't lift boxes all day like I did; she would empty boxes into her cart, then take the cart around to stock the items. One of the managers told her to stop; those carts were for customers to use, not her. She tried to tell him that she was more efficient this way, she could take four or five boxes at a time, instead of one or two pieces. He wouldn't listen and told me to handle the situation. Super Cee was very upset, but I thought of a loophole. The return desk would sort items by area and put them in carts to be restocked. I told her to trick him; keep using the cart, and if he saw her, she was to tell him that she was putting away the customer returns from the return desk. She was happy to do it. Every time she saw him, she gave him a big smile and told him she was restocking the returns. He never said another word about the cart.

After I left for the day, the evening shipment of new merchandise would be unloaded to be stocked overnight. Super Cee was supposed to spend the last few hours of her shift straightening up the sales floor and making sure everything was neat. She and I did that as we worked, so she preferred to go back and get the new stock and start putting it out right away. She was told that was not her job; she was to be making the sales floor look nice. Since she had already done that, she felt she had nothing to do for half her shift. I told her to use the cart again; go back and un-box things and put them in her cart. If asked, she should say she was re-stocking returns, I promised no one would be the wiser. It worked, and she was happy to be kept busy her whole shift, and I was happy to come in and find the new stock had been worked properly. We were a great team; I wouldn't have traded her for anyone.

Every retail store must keep a close eye on their inventory. It is a vital part of successfully running a business, keeping a good balance of inventory. You need to have products for customers to buy but don't want to tie up your bottom line holding too many products in storage. Some smaller stores do a monthly inventory, while large chains usually do a yearly inventory. Monthly would ensure your inventory would stay more accurate, but it's not feasible in a large store with millions of dol-lars of products on hand. Every year, each store in the company goes through an inventory. These are scheduled almost a year in advance. Every store manager I worked under had a different system to get the store ready. Some started months before, while some waited till the last minute. Home office would send out guidelines and timetables to fol-low to get ready, but they were rarely used. Some guidelines applied to the whole store, while some were area specific. As you would expect, the earlier you started to prep, the smoother the inventory went. The prep on the sales floor was pretty standard; you would go through each aisle and shelf and make sure that each item was in its correct place. In the back room, you would open each box, make a shelf label of the item in-side, and stick that on the box with the quantity. It's really not hard, just frustrating when someone messes up what you have done and you have to do it again. And again. And again. I preferred to prep my area myself; that way I knew it was done correctly. Many times, I spent days getting my back room area ready, only to go home and come in the next morn-ing to find it a shambles. New products had come in, and instead of just leaving them for me to prep, someone rearranged my whole space, re-moved labels, and crossed out counts. Needless to say, I was pretty mad that I had to start over, even angrier when the store manager came by to yell at me because my area was not ready. When you finished prepping your area, you would be directed to help others who were behind. The area that always need the most help was clothing. It took forever to prep because you had to make a label for each piece of clothing (and there is a lot, no matter how well you run the area).

Many years I worked sixteen- to eighteen-hour days the week of inventory, helping to prep clothing. Certain areas could not be prepped early, as it sold way too quickly. Food, toilet paper, detergent, beauty, and hygiene had to be done just days before. The last two weeks before inventory are long on overtime and short on patience. Two days before inventory, some of the state team would come in to inspect the store, and they always found things that had to be redone. Sometimes they would just decide that even though you had followed the home office guideline, they didn't like it and would want it changed. Then an argument would start about who was right, home office or the state team. Since no one from the home office was there to back you up in person, the state team would win, and you'd have to redo what should have been finished and ready. No matter how carefully you prepped your area, you could bet they would find something for you to change, even if they had to make up a reason to change it.

The months, weeks, and days leading up to inventory become more and more hectic until the fateful day arrives. That day is one of two days that everyone in retail hates. One is Black Friday, the busiest day of the year, and one is inventory, the longest and most boring. A special crew is hired to come in and count every item in the store while we all stand around and watch. You aren't allowed to touch anything while they work. You can't put items that customers have moved back where they belong because the item could be counted twice. You would hang out and chat with your friends, watching the counting crew and noting how many mistakes they were making. You were not allowed to point out a mistake; if they missed counting a whole aisle, you were to call the store manager, and he was to get with one of their supervisors.

One of the crew was supposed to come back and count what had been missed, but that rarely happened. Once they called an area done, there was no going back. Many times, we watched as one of the crew counted all the towels on a display together. The towels had been carefully separated by color, style, and UPC code. The crew knew that each UPC was to be counted if the inventory was to be accurate, but there will always be people who are careless. Those kinds of mistakes happened all over the store. It was very frustrating to watch all your hard work go down the drain over carelessness that you were powerless to stop as time dragged by. The next day, you would try to correct the counting mistakes and then take down all the little tags the counting crew had stuck everywhere. Then it was back to business as usual for another year.

My only minor headache in the bedding area was my lead. He was one of those people who was born to supervise, not actually do the work. He was over home goods, household, paint, and crafts. He was annoying because he would not help you with anything; he considered his job to delegate any notes to us and then come back every fifteen minutes to see if you were done. Since he wasn't actually doing any work himself, he had all the time in the world to check up on you. Every day in the afternoon is cleanup time; everyone on the floor is supposed to stop and spend an hour cleaning up their area and putting away misplaced items. I was doing that one day when he stopped by and just stood there watching me. After a few minutes, I asked him if he needed something, and he said he had stopped to remind me that it was cleanup time.

I was confused. "What does it look like I'm doing?"

"It looks like you might be doing the cleanup."

"Good guess, since that is what I am doing. You needed to ask?" Now I was really confused.

"It is my job to check on my areas and make sure they are doing their tasks," he explained. "That's why I am asking if you are doing the cleanup."

I stopped and looked at him. "You couldn't tell by the way I am re-folding the towels and putting the colors back together? Have you gotten that unfamiliar with the process? Feel free to jump in and get some practice," I said sarcastically.

Apparently, I hurt his feelings. "There is no need to be rude to me. This is part of my job. I am supposed to ask these things," he said defensively.

I gave a big sigh. "Well, since you have asked, I am doing exactly what it looks like. I am cleaning up my area and putting away misplaced items. Thank you for checking in on me." I was crossing into rudeness but was tired of his micromanaging.

"Why are you having such an attitude and talking to me like I am an idiot?" His temper was rising.

I had a choice now. I could smile and try to defuse the situation or just let him have it. Most times, I don't say what I am thinking and spare the other person's feelings. But sometimes you've just had enough, and you let the words fly.

"Well, one of us in this conversation doesn't seem that smart. And I don't think it's me." We stared at each other for a few seconds before he walked away. I went back to work and didn't see him the rest of the day. When he came around the next day to ask if I was doing the cleanup, I just said "Yep!" and smiled at him. He nodded, and after that, he never asked me again. I took it as a small victory.

No matter how large the store or how many employees on the payroll, it doesn't take long to get to know almost everyone who works the same shift. Some you like, some you can't stand, and some you just tolerate. I've worked with hundreds if not thousands of people; most I don't remember at all, but some I'll never forget. A woman I became good friends with was Fran. Her area was home entertainment—TVs and such. I met her when I got my first area; we got promoted about the same time. She had grown up in California, but we were both from low-/middle-class households and shared similar stories from childhood; handed-down clothes, leftovers every night, playing in the yard, and strict parents. We were both familiar with the rule of "we don't have money for that, so make do with what you have." But where she had rice and beans most nights, we did have beef, since we raised cattle and butchered every year. And the games were different. She played in the street with the other kids on the block; my brother and I played two-man baseball in the backyard. Only farm kids understand pausing the game to look for the ball in the wheat field. But she and I shared the same work ethic and desire to take pride in our work.

She often joined us for lunch, and we welcomed her, but not her girlfriend, who also worked at the store. She and Fran were a couple for at least ten years when her girlfriend broke things off in a very public and hurtful way. I had been giving Fran a ride home from work for over a year. She had no car, and we left at the same time, so I didn't mind. I spent many months just listening and trying to console her after the breakup, trying to be a good friend. No matter what I thought of her relationship, she was a friend, and she was hurting. We spent many hours talking it out, with her trying to understand why she had been treated so and me trying to convince her that she had done nothing to deserve this; in fact she deserved much better. Often, we would sit in my car outside her place and just talk about life. We also shared a love of ice cream, and some summer days we would stop and get a cone to enjoy on the way home. My friendship with her taught me a lot about how to have respectful conversations with others.

She left retail a number of years ago, but we still talk often and get together when we can, sharing laughs about our old times at work. One story we still laugh about was very embarrassing for me. When I worked in bedding, I was gathering boxes of pillows to be stocked on the floor. The boxes are very large but light, easy to lift but you can't see around them where you are going. I stepped up onto a pallet and grabbed a box, then turned to walk back to my rolling cart so I could take it and other boxes to the sales floor. I forgot where the edge of the pallet was, missed the step, and fell forward to the floor. Now, a pallet is only about five inches high, so I didn't fall very far. Apparently, my body didn't agree; my bladder must have thought I'd just jumped out of an airplane and was in free fall. When I hit the floor, something between my bladder and brain screamed "Evacuate!" I lay there a moment and then realized that I had just peed my pants. I quickly got up, hoping no one had seen me and would come to help. I hurried to the bathroom, praying no one would see me or notice anything. At least it wasn't running down my leg, making a trail to follow. In the stall, I surveyed the state of my jeans and had to decide if I would go home and change or stay at work and hope I dried quickly. If I wanted to go home, I would have to go to management and explain why. I was way too embarrassed to do that, so I came up with a plan. I would go to the air fresheners and spray some Febreze on myself to cover the smell and hope my clothes would dry faster. I did so and within an hour felt pretty dry and not so self-conscious. I went and told my story to my friend Fran. She laughed but had sympathy and promised not to tell anyone else. She had a sensitive stomach, and if her lunch did not agree with her, she would have to make a hasty trip to the bathroom. Some days, she would come back and tell me how she almost didn't make it before her body had to "evacuate," and we'd laugh again.

9

About two years later, I made another move. Patsy had left the company, and I was asked to move back to claims, as it is a two-person job. The man who was working with Patsy wanted to take her spot, but I had previous experience. I decided not to put in for the supervisor job and let him have it instead. I felt it wasn't worth causing hurt feelings if I got promoted ahead of him. Ned and I got along fine; he was very friendly and easygoing. Everyone in the store liked him—that is, until they had to work with him. Ned could be very lazy. He spent the first hour of the day just getting coffee, greeting all his friends, and checking his email. He was happy to let me do 90 percent of the work while he sat at the computer.

Every hour, he would get up on the pretense of "checking on something" as he walked around and talked with friends and got more coffee. His shift was 7 a.m. to 4 p.m., and at three forty, I would announce it was "Ned time," meaning time for him to start cleaning up his desk area, putting his handheld scanner away, and throwing away his coffee cups. I would keep working till my shift ended at 6 p.m. After he left, I could finally get on the computer and check my emails and process my paperwork for the day. I didn't really mind; I usually can't stand lazy people, but at least he was pleasant and took my comments about how little he did in stride. When I noted that he seemed to have accomplished absolutely nothing all day, he just smiled. I don't know if he thought I was joking and really thought he was working hard or if he knew he was lazy and just didn't care. I have worked with plenty who consider themselves hard workers who barely get any work done. Some people just have no idea what hard work really is; one person's 100 percent is another's 10.

Everyone knew who got the bulk of the work done; anytime I went on vacation, I would come back to a disaster area. Once I took a three-day weekend and came back to nineteen shopping carts full of broken or damaged merchandise to process. Ned's vacation started the day I got back, so I would have to clean up claims myself. It took me ten minutes just to move the carts so I could enter the office and get my handheld scanner to start work. That kind of mess can make some people paralyzed, but I remind myself of the old kids' joke: How do you eat an elephant? One bite at a time. Just pick up one thing, process it, and then pick up the next thing and keep going. I have found it the only effective way of dealing with an overwhelming situation. I just kept working, and by lunch, I had about five carts left; by the end of the day, all the carts were gone, and I had started making a dent on everything that was piled on the floor. I had the office back to normal in a few days, but it was a ton of work.

Ned was helpful for some things. The main thing he was good for was lifting heavy items out of the shopping carts for me. I am strong enough to lift most things but am short and cannot always lift a sixty-pound floor safe up and out of a shopping cart. Ned would do that much, complaining about how I was killing him with all this work I was asking him to do. I was full of sympathy and told him he should probably get some more coffee and take a break. He agreed, ignoring my sarcasm.

A couple of times a year, we would get a compliance visit from head office. Someone would come in and inspect our work and make sure we were following company protocols. Usually the same man would come to all the stores in the state, so I got to know him and was friendly and joked with him. As a result, if he found something wrong, he would give me a chance to fix it instead of reporting it immediately. On one visit, he was going through his checklist while Ned and I were both in the room. Ned liked to be gone on visit days and let me handle the whole thing, but this time he was there. The man started asking questions about who handled this and that, and each time, Ned said, "Oh, that's Julie's job." Finally, the man asked Ned just exactly what his job was, since I seemed to be doing all the work. I found this quite amusing, since it was true; Ned did not. The compliance officer reported his findings to the manager, and Ned was called down to the managers' office and told he needed to step up and do more, since he was the supervisor. His opinion was that as the supervisor, he had the power to delegate tasks but was reminded that he didn't get to delegate *every* task. Ned helped out more after that, doing any heavy lifting and prepping boxes for shipping.

I worked with Ned for a couple of years before I got tired of the daily dump-and-run problem. I guess people think that it shouldn't be a big deal to drop off one item. But they forget that the whole store does it. Broken mirrors are left lying face down so when you pick them up, shards fly all over you. Someone tosses a bottle of shampoo without a lid in a tub, and it leaks, making everything inside a gross mess. Moldy food gets left instead of throwing it out and just leaving the package. Every single day I would clean the mess up, go home, and the next day do it again. After a while, it wears on you, and you either move or become very cranky. So, I moved out to work in clothing, one area I never thought I would run. I found it interesting that after I left, Ned ended up with three employees working under him, and he would still complain that they didn't get as much done as I had. Guess I left big shoes to fill.

10

There is one day in retail more dreaded than any other. Black Friday is not for the faint of heart. My guess is those people who love to go Black Friday shopping have never had to work one, especially at a large retail store. It all starts early in October, as the extra freight starts rolling in. The back room becomes more and more crowded, and soon it's just a maze of pallets and displays you must navigate to get from one end to the other. The freight just keeps coming, well after the store is bursting at the seams. The last batch to arrive comes on a special semi-trailer that is left docked at the store. It is unloaded and everything sorted and processed and then reloaded to store the merchandise until the sale. There's no room to move, much less work effectively.

Maps of where each item is to be displayed for the big night are drawn and redrawn daily. Home office will send their official map, but it must be adjusted for each store's space and floor plan. Home office also sends down detailed instructions of where each item should go, how it should be displayed, and a complete game plan of how to run the store for the sale. Reality is never so neat and easy. While home office would have you believe their playbook is the Bible, most store managers use it as a guideline, and some barely use it at all.

Employees are given assignments for the night; some are to run a register, some are to guard displays until the sale starts, and some get the joy of monitoring and handing out high priced items of limited quantity. Some of the men will be assigned to load large items into customers' cars. The large-item pickup usually happens on the side of the building, hopefully out of traffic flow. They load up trampolines, large-screen televisions, and any other items that would be hazardous to move through the crowded store.

We watch as the pallets keep piling up in the back room. Displays are shuffled around, trying to gain and inch here or a foot there. Everything has to be sorted, all the TVs must be stacked by size and brand, the pillows and towels grouped together, and the toys rounded up and ready to be displayed. The toys are the most hated area; no one wants to be the poor schmuck assigned to guard the season's hot item. We only get a handful of the sought-after toy, but of course, no quantity would be enough to satisfy the demanding horde. Hot-ticket items are usually handled by seasoned employees, those with experience from years past. It doesn't hurt to put someone unpleasant in charge of the line; they probably won't get their feelings hurt easily and won't be making friends anyway.

The day of the sale is spent flushing all the merchandise out of the back room and onto the sales floor. The person in charge is never the same person who drew up the last version of the map, so nothing is in its assigned home. This causes quite a mess later as the customers are given a map of where items are displayed, but few are in the proper location. As items are displayed, employees start the exciting task of "guarding" the pallets. You are supposed to keep customers from tearing open the shrink wrap and helping themselves to items before the sale starts. Mostly we would stand in little groups, talking as managers hurried by, trying to figure out where everything was and why nothing was where it should be. I'd usually take a lap around the store and get a feel of where the most sought-after items were, so I could at least point customers in the right direction.

As the hours before the sale ticked by, more customers started coming in and staking out the store. Customers fit into one of three groups: (1) This is a fun family tradition! (Those who are very organized with lists, ads, and walkie-talkies); (2) Everyone better get out of my way! (Those who want only two items that are on different sides of the store and are pissed about that fact); and (3) I don't actually want to buy anything. I just came to enjoy the show. (They cause the most disruption, pushing people for no reason and shoplifting what they can.)

Once customers found the item they couldn't live without, they would mark their territory by almost any means. Thankfully, in all my years, I never actually saw someone mark their spot by peeing on the floor, but I'd hardly be surprised if it did happen. What most did was go get some folding camp chairs from sporting goods and take a seat in the line. Then, as the wait stretched on, one of their group (you never go Black Friday shopping alone; you need the whole entourage with you) would go to the deli counter and get snacks. The snacks were rarely paid for, just taken back to the line and eaten, along with the bottles of pop from the front-end coolers. This trend of helping yourself to refreshments has gotten increasingly worse over the years.

As the hour grows closer, the swarm of customers increases. The aisles became impassable, clogged with customers and shopping carts until you could hardly shoulder your way through to the bathroom. The half hour before the sale starts is the worst bit of waiting. Those who have been holding their place in lines are now sick of waiting and lash out any newcomers who try to push in. Patience is long gone, and the friendly chit-chat is now angry grumbling. The store sounds like a beehive, a constant droning hum. Sometimes the store manager would get on the intercom and make announcements, which is a complete waste, as it was impossible to hear what was said. As the minutes ticked down the tensions went up. Everyone checked their watches compulsively as they pressed closer and closer to the items they were waiting for. Many years, I guarded pallets on the floor, waiting for the sale to start, so I could unwrap the items and then try to get out of the way without getting crushed. As the customers and I waited, I learned what to say to try to keep the crowd calm and compliant.

"All I want to do is just remove this wrap and let you get the items. I want you to buy these things and take them home because I never want to see them again. Just let me have a minute to do my job, so you can get on with your shopping."

It worked pretty well. Most people would move slightly so I could take my position, ready to go at zero hour. The sale never actually started at the exact time; within the last ten minutes, someone somewhere in the store would just start grabbing items. That would start a chain reaction that ran through the store like a rolling wave. Even without hearing the announcements overhead, you would know it had started by the noise level. The droning hum suddenly rose to a deafening, frenzied buzzing. You had to move quickly. Cut the wrapping, try to pull it out of the way, and move back as best you could as the crowd surged forward, then move on to the next display. In mere seconds, the store was chaos; voices yelling, carts crashing into everything, merchandise being tossed back and forth, and employees ducking for cover. Once you could move, your main goal was to get off the floor and to the safety of the back room. There you would wait for ten to fifteen minutes. By that time, some of the crowd had gotten what they had come for and were now storming the checkouts. Lines backed up immediately, the carts creating a traffic jam worse than 5 p.m. Friday rush hour. Now that some of the horde had moved to the front of the store, it was safer to venture out of the back room. We'd come out of hiding and work our way through the debris field. Indeed, it looked like a tornado had swept through the building. Displays empty and overturned, wrap tangled everywhere, pallets strewn along the floor with items discarded on top. We would start stacking up empty pallets, gathering wrap and destroyed cardboard displays, and haul it all to the back room, then come back for more. Unless you were cashiering or still handing out items in a line, all hands were needed for the cleanup. Abandoned carts of random items that were shoved in every corner of the sales floor had to be collected and merchandise put back in place.

As you collected a sale item that had been grabbed and then dropped, another customer would come and take it out of your hands, dump it in their cart, and rush off. As we worked our way around the store, we would also collect the camp chairs that had been snagged (some now broken from the crowd) and gather the empty pop bottles and food wrappers stuffed under the chairs, the contents consumed but never paid for. We would pass each other, arms loaded heading to the back room, arms empty coming back for more, just silently shaking our heads at the destruction. The second wave came within an hour; customers who had been at other stores now came to ours to see what was left. We were constantly stopped and asked what was left and where would they find it. We tried to be civil when all we really wanted to do was yell for them to get out and stay out. It usually took two to three hours to put most of the store back together, a depressing thought, since it had taken no more than fifteen minutes to tear it apart. When the register lines finally cleared out, we would breathe a sigh of relief and groups would start collecting in the break room to compare notes. Who had been yelled at, pushed, or shoved; who had witnessed an actual fight; who had seen someone taken out in handcuffs. The new hires would sit quietly, looking shell shocked. Most said the same thing: "I'd been Black Friday shopping before but had no idea it was like this." Not surprisingly, many quit soon after.

11

Clothing is an area that intimidates most employees. Customers see an orderly layout of walls, racks, and tables filled with sized and color-coded displays. Employees see a tangled rainbow forest where they may get lost forever. Any piece of clothing found in another part of the store is quickly brought back and dumped at the fitting room. There is a system to how and where pieces are displayed, but most never understand it. Each section (or pad) is separated; men's, women's, boys', girls', and infants'. And each pad has its own layout, separating casual from dress wear from sleepwear. Each type is sized and color-coded. Just when you have it set properly, it is time to change it all for the next season. Seasonal change happens four times a year, and a total reset happens at least once. The reset means switching the types around within the pad; shifting the walls, racks, and tables.

Each day is spent putting pieces back where they belong, putting out new pieces from the back room, and processing the price changes sent from home office. Other areas would have items go on clearance at the end of a season or at a modular change, three hundred price changes to work was considered quite a task. But clothing had thousands to work each season; each color and size had to be done individually. Some found it terrifying to deal with, but as with almost everything in retail, it's just about having a system. It is much easier to go through each rack of clothes than to try to find each item listed on the scanner one at a time. Usually clothes go on clearance at season change, so if it is changing from spring to summer, check through all the spring items to see if they are being reduced. It takes some time but is much easier than criss-crossing the whole area looking for one piece at a time.

The best times in retail are when you get to work with people who have your same work ethic. It's a blessing to know you can rely on your coworkers to pull their own weight and even help you if needed. I have been very fortunate to work with a few such people over the years, and most have become lifelong friends. In the clothing area, I made two new friends, Chick and Vic. They had worked together for a year or so in clothing and were very friendly and helped me learn the ropes. Vic had a very loud and distinctive laugh; you could hear her from almost anywhere in the store. Chick and I loved to be silly and get her laughing; other employees would come by just to see what was going on that was so funny. Vic would get very embarrassed, but we kept it up anyway. We kept each other laughing as we worked through the never-ending workload. Chick and Vic were both hard working, so together we pushed a lot of clothing from the back room to the floor. Clothing can get out of control really quickly. Since it is all imported, you get a ton dumped on you at once, then nothing, then a ton more when the next shipment comes in. You have to keep up with it, or it will become a monster.

Each year as our areas reset, Chick, Vic, and I would go overnights to help each other get it done. Another woman who ran the jewelry counter also helped; we liked her and were glad to have her. Our area lead also would say she was going to help, but mostly she wanted to get away from any manager watching her and screw around with no supervision. We started on Sunday night to redo my area; we had only been working about thirty minutes when the lead announced that she had to leave. Her daughter was pregnant, and supposedly her water had broken, so she had to go take the daughter to the hospital right now. None of us minded; we knew the lead wasn't going to do much work anyway.

Her true talent was in spreading gossip and avoiding work. We continued working and didn't think much about it except that none of us were surprised that she found a reason to leave work. The next night, we all came in again and picked up where each of us had left off. I had finished what the lead had started instead of leaving it a mess; she fussed at me that I should have just left it, since she had planned to do it now. I had no intention of leaving any of my area half-done at the end of my shift; it just would have given her something else to complain about. So, she started on a new area, tearing it apart, and had just made a big mess when she announced that again she would have to leave and go see about her daughter. We asked what was wrong, and she said her water had broken and she was having contractions. We just looked at each other confused; hadn't her water broken the day before? She told us that she had two water bags, and now that the second one had broken, she would have the baby tonight.

She left, and we spent the rest of the night laughing and debating the possibility of two water bags, as none of us had ever heard of such a thing. We had a good laugh about it and did not see the lead the rest of the week, which suited all of us just fine. We finished the work and spent the rest of the week coming up with the most outlandish excuses for missing work that we could think of. Our friend from the jewelry counter was from India, and I told her that she should call in next weekend saying that her brother in India had fought against the Taliban and was a national hero, and she was flying back for the celebration and parade in his honor. Every time the lead had some crazy new excuse for missing work, I would ask my friend how the parade for her brother had been. We laughed about it for a long time.

Another season change found the four of us working overnights again doing resets. Thankfully, the lead decided that this time she needed to stay on days, since most of her team was overnight. We didn't miss her and definitely didn't need her. The four of us worked quickly and worked our way through the areas with no trouble. There was only one manager who worked overnights, handing out tasks and notes to the regular overnight crew. He would come and check on us too, mostly to see what all the laughing was about. The four of us had a great time joking back and forth as we worked. He couldn't believe that we could be productive and have fun at the same time. He was a tall, middle-aged man who would stomp through the store talking to no one but glaring at everyone. Most employees were either afraid of him or just thought he was a complete jerk and avoided him. Our last night, we joined forces to reset bras; they are always a big mess and take the longest to sort out. The girls were teasing me, insisting that I was his favorite since he had stopped and spoken to me every night but no one else. Vic claimed that he had been looking for me the night before, checking every aisle till he saw me. She said it reminded her of a dog tracking its prey. She told me to howl at the moon and see if he appeared, he would come and answer the mating call. I said no way, so she howled at the ceiling instead. Immediately he poked his head around the aisle and asked what on earth we were doing. We all lost it, the four of us doubled over, laughing till we cried. He just stood there and stared at us till I finally caught my breath and told him that Vic was just telling us a funny story about her dog. He looked doubtful but eventually walked away. The others finally calmed down enough to get back to work, but one would start giggling again, and then we would all start up. We never saw him again the rest of the night.

Chick and I were trying to get winter coats under control one year. There were so many of every size that we used an extra storage area in the back room and set up long bars suspended from chains. We had tiers of bars to maximize the space; you could only reach the highest bar by standing on a ladder. The lower two tiers were full, so Chick was on the ladder, and I was bringing her armfuls of coats to hang on the bars. The bars were really close together, so I had to push my way through the lower coats to bring more to Chick. As I struggled to get to her with another armful, I could hear her laughing hysterically. When I got to her, she was laughing so hard she was crying, and I started laughing too, even though I didn't know what was so funny. She finally could tell me that as I made my way to her, she couldn't see me at all, just the coats moving as I pushed past. She remembered the scene in *Jurassic Park 2*, when the little girl is up on the high platform, watching the trees sway beneath her as the T-Rexes passed. We both started laughing again, barely able to stop. The best part of the joke was how I always complained about being unable to reach things because of my short T-Rex arms—now I really was the T-Rex! Every time we stocked coats that winter, we would laugh about it again.

Chick, Vic, and I were the three musketeers, even when Vic moved to run the toy area. We would go to lunch together every day; we would leave the building and go out to eat, just to get a break from work. You can stay and eat in the break room, but if you brought your lunch, it was often stolen out of the fridge, leaving you nothing to eat, and then you also got to listen to all the calls about your area the whole time. Plus, as an added bonus, you could listen to someone telling their drama to the whole room, recounting how there was a drunken party at their house and Grandma had gotten arrested. (No lie, I actually walked into the break room one day, and an employee was telling that story to at least a dozen people. I turned and walked back out, deciding I didn't need a break that badly.) So, we chose to go out and get away from every-one. We would often walk to the warehouse store next door and eat at the snack bar. It was the cheapest lunch in town—pizza slice and a drink for three dollars or hot dog and drink for two dollars. You had to watch the pizza, though, and make sure it hadn't been sitting too long, or you would spend half your afternoon in the bathroom with the gurgles. That is what Vic called it, when you ate something greasy, and about half an hour later, your stomach started gurgling, and you knew you had better get to the bathroom quick. Once Chick, Vic, and I took two other friends out for lunch; we couldn't decide on what to eat and ended up at the cheapest taco place in town. After we got back to work, within an hour we all ended up in the bathroom at the same time, all having an attack of the gurgles. We all laughed as we took turns in the stalls, hoping we weren't going to back up the toilets!

While I was working in clothing, I started to have a lot of foot prob-lems. My feet hurt constantly; taking the first few steps out of bed in the morning were almost unbearable. I asked about who any of my friends knew and liked to treat foot pain and made my first appointment with a podiatrist. Unfortunately, I have gotten to know him and his staff very well over the years. He diagnosed me with plantar fasciitis and bone spurs in both feet. I bought new shoes and had to start using night splints to hold my feet in a certain position while I slept. I also got to experience my first cortisone shot; I've had many more since, each just as painful as the last. I had waited too long to see him, and the damage was done and required surgery. I had both feet done that year, bone spurs scraped off and a notch cut in the tendon to stretch it and ease the inflammation. I was off work for five weeks with the first surgery in the spring and six weeks with the second in the fall. It did help, but my doctor warned I'd be seeing him again if I continued working on my feet. I told him I didn't have much choice, but I would start working toward getting out of retail.

12

At the time of my foot surgeries, a position in the human resources office came open. I went to the manager and told him I was putting in for it. I had tried to get a position in that office in the past but was told I was too valuable on the floor to let me move. But we had a new manager now, so I went to him and said I would like the job. The other woman in the office was Diana, known as the Dragon Lady; she had chewed up and spit out her last three assistants. But of course, I had known her for years, as we had both worked in the store. This manager told me the same thing as the last manager: he didn't want to lose me on the floor because of my experience. I could go help any area—set modulars, process price changes, and help clean up areas in trouble. I told him that refusing to move me might help him, but it certainly wasn't helping me. I felt it was very unfair and asked him if anyone else trying for the job had my experience and knowledge of company policies. He admitted that no one else did, and Diana agreed that of those who had put their names in, I was her first choice. I moved to the HR office and into the most challenging area I have ever worked. It definitely tested my belief that I can learn anything.

There was a ton to learn. Files, payroll, tracking hours, applications and orientation classes, leave-of-absence claims, insurance questions, timeclock problems, call-ins, and terminations. Everything from hiring to firing, with every conceivable question in between. Diana was about fifteen years older and was very old school. She did not believe in starting at the shallow end and learning to tread water; she threw you right off a cliff into the ocean and told you to make your way back to shore.

She didn't accept excuses for anything. Even good reasons were not good enough for her; you had better do it right the first time or you would be doing it again and again. I spent my days on the computer and phone, which seemed to never stop ringing. We each had a phone at our desks, and if she was already on hers and it rang again, I was to transfer that call to mine and answer it immediately. My multitasking skills were stretched to the limit, as I was often on the phone and helping an employee who had come into the office with a question at the same time. And of course, as soon as one employee came to the door, a line would start to form. Then the manager would come in the other door and want one of us to look something up or send an email for him. I had never had to use the company email before this; we were all supposed to check it, but few on the sales floor ever did. I hated it immediately; it was not user friendly at all.

Trying to add someone to my address book was a twenty-step process, and I had no time for that. Searching for people was ridiculous; if you didn't know their full name and spell it correctly, you never found them. But if someone emailed you, they were saved automatically. So, I was desperate for anyone to email me, so I didn't have to try to add them, only to find out later it hadn't saved that contact after all. I had to use the email daily, cursing it every time. At first Diana found this very annoying, but she soon found it amusing to tell me to email the whole store about the upcoming insurance meeting, or a cookout celebrating some holiday. Then she would sit back and smile as I cursed the email system for an hour, fighting it the whole time. Then when I finally finished, (or at least told her I had; I had sent her an email, and she couldn't tell if I had sent one to everyone else or not), she would tell me that

I should put up a notice at the timeclock, in case some people didn't check their email. She would then smile the most evil, wicked smile and announce it was time for her lunch, leaving the room before I could explode. She wasn't called the Dragon Lady for nothing.

Diana wasn't all evil; she could be very compassionate and would do all she could to help out employees in need. She was a very tough, no-nonsense person who knew her job inside and out. She rarely made mistakes and expected me to follow her standard. I already knew all this, having worked around her for years. Her learning curve was more of a vertical cliff; she would show me something once and expect that I understood and would not need to be shown again. I feel I learn pretty quickly and picked up on the everyday things without any trouble, but HR has a thousand things that you need to know how to do. And some things only come up once every blue moon, which meant you really had to dig to find out how to handle those situations. Diana often took care of those herself, not trusting me, which I did not mind; she piled plenty on my plate each day.

One responsibility she gave me was to try to keep the employees current on their computer training. Quizzes were downloaded for each employee to take regularly; new hires spent two days getting them done. Some quizzes had to be taken yearly by everyone, even managers. These were not optional but assigned to everyone in the company by home office. Every week I would print out the list and try to round up employees to get them done. The supervisors and managers were the worst, always complaining of being too busy. I would remind them that I had been in their shoes and ask if they could just do one quiz a day until they were caught up. Most would try without too much argument, but one manager fought me every time I brought it up. He was over store safety and security, and since the quizzes were about workplace safety, you would think he would just do them. But after I spoke to him about it three times, he became irritated and told me to stop bothering him. He said if doing the quizzes was not on his weekly checklist from the state safety officer, he wasn't going to do them. I told him that I understood, and after he left the room, I emailed the state safety officer and asked if he could kindly add completing the quizzes to his weekly checklist. It worked. That manager came to me the next week very angry, complaining that I had gotten him in trouble, and he would make me sorry. I very calmly asked him if that was a threat (since threats are, of course, against company policy) and informed him that if he took any disciplinary action against me, I would report him. I hadn't been intimidated by any manager when I was a new hire, and I had no intention of being intimidated by anyone now. He stormed off and didn't speak to me again, which was fine with me.

Each year we had to do a file review. That meant pulling the file on each employee and going through a checklist to make sure all the proper forms were included and that each had been properly filled out. Any missing or incomplete forms had to be redone, and then the file was checked off as complete. It was a big task and took three months to finish. One of the forms I had to check was a current pay sheet, listing the employees' last job review and raise. As I went through the file on a certain woman, I checked her sheet and saw that she had received an above standard on her last review, and I had gotten a standard rating. I was furious. She was very lazy, and I had personally bailed out her area on two occasions. She certainly didn't earn that rating and raise through hard work. When review time came around, 1 percent of the store got an above, 1 percent got a below, and the rest were given a standard. I was already angry that I busted my ass just to be lumped in with the 98 percent, but this really rubbed salt in that wound. I finally calmed down, reminding myself that I cannot control others, only my actions and reactions. I have had to tell myself that many times over the years, since crap like that happens all the time. Favoritism happens constantly; people are promoted or given raises for laughing at the manager's jokes. Others keep their heads down and work hard but are passed over time and time again. It is very easy to adopt a permanent bad attitude when you see things like this happening, but in the end, that does you no good. Your bad attitude won't change the situation you are upset about and only makes every tough situation worse. It was a hard lesson to learn, but I had to let go of my anger and focus on my work and doing my best each day.

Each store I have worked in has been its own soap opera. There are no secrets in retail; the building is filled with dramas and scandals. There are always one or two gossips. If you want a rumor to be spread, just tell one of them, and the whole place will know by the end of your shift. Some people just feed on that; they cannot keep anything to themselves. Others invent stories to hurt coworkers or make themselves look good; they are happiest when they can do both at the same time. I try to stay away from both types; it just makes for an uncomfortable work environment when you are in the middle of the drama. I'm not sure who first said "silence cannot be misquoted," but I have followed that wisdom many times and never been sorry. I have been called unfriendly and rude for not joining in the store rumor mill and have never been sorry about that either.

One of my primary jobs in HR was to bring in the new hires and lead them through job orientation. It took most of my shift, so I would try to work with six to ten people at a time. I had them fill out all their paperwork and watch videos about basic job requirements and safety. I don't know how some were able to fill out an application online. Someone (probably Mommy) must have helped, because when it came to filling out basic information forms, they could barely write their name. They also had to bring in a photo ID and social security card; they were told this at least three times before the actual day of orientation. I still had a few come in without them, and I would have to send them home. They could either get them and come back or get called for the next class. Once, I sent the group to take a break and stretch their legs, and one of the new hires just left and never came back. I also had a couple sit through the whole thing and never come back for a second day of work. Most would work for a few weeks, maybe a month, and then quit; some made it six months; very few made it a whole year. If they made it the first year, they would probably stay long term, but that percentage is very low.

I had a big handbook from the home office spelling out everything I was to do for the class, word for word. If you followed the book, the class would take almost two eight-hour days. I shrank that to about six hours total, as I skipped or took shortcuts through a lot. First of all, I was way too busy to dedicate two whole days to doing nothing but the class. Second, the book was written as if we were hiring first graders. I admit some seemed to be at that level of learning, but it was an insult to the intelligence of everyone else. And I was sure that if I treated all of them like they were stupid, no one would stay any time at all. Third, there was no way I could read the whole book word for word; I'd die of boredom myself before I finished. So, I gave my abridged version, highlighting the important bits. If I had read it all as printed, each page would take five minutes, my way took about one. So, I breezed through it, knowing that those with intelligence got the point and those without never would. Besides the paperwork took long enough, some I would have to explain each section to because they did not understand some of the words. And of course, I was still interrupted often; some employee always needed something. Diana would insist I lead the class because she didn't want to but then would complain when she had to help people instead of sending them to me. Some came to me anyway since they didn't want to deal with her.

The first headache was getting all the paperwork filled out properly; the second was the computer work. The young kids could barely put a pen to paper, and the older folks close to retirement age had never used a computer before. I had one poor older man just sit in front of the computer; he had never touched one in his life. I had to show him how to use the mouse, how when he moved it around, that caused the little arrow on the screen to move too. Then he had to hover over things and click on them, but he was so nervous that his hands keep shaking, and he would click the wrong thing. Of course, others in the class needed my help too. Fran stopped by and said hi, and I begged her to help him while I got the rest on track. She did and very patiently walked him through the basics of point and click. He finally got the hang of it and was grateful; he never failed to say hello to her every day after that. I tried to have patience with all the new hires; I worked with every age and education level there is. One young man knew how to use the computer but could barely read. Each employee had to fill out a W4 for their tax withholdings. Most had no idea what to do but could figure it out with a little help. I had to read the whole thing to this young man and show him where to put in his information. At the end, you complete it with a digital signature by typing AGREE in the final box. The screen actually says that—type AGREE here. So, I told him that's what he needed to do, and he just sat there. I went to help someone else and came back to see him still not done. When I asked him what was wrong, he finally said he didn't know how to spell *agree*, even though it was right on the screen in front of him. I told him, and he finally finished and left for the day. I just shook my head and wondered how on earth he had graduated.

I am always amazed at how many people claim to be adults but have never left the high school mindset. I heard a ton of drama while in HR, more than I cared to hear in my whole life. Grown people coming to me and whining because they think someone doesn't like them because they moved away from them in the break room. (It obviously had nothing to do with the fact that the whiner had a cold.) So and so leaves the area when I walk in. (Have you tried taking a shower?) The whole meat department was talking together, but everyone shut up when they saw me. (They were wondering when you would be fired for calling in six times this month.) The parade of whiners never stopped; employees, supervisors, even managers came to the office to try to find a sympathetic shoulder to cry on. Unfortunately for them, I am not a very sympathetic person.

One supervisor came to the office and complained very loudly how he had far too much work to do and one of his two helpers had been pulled to help another area whose helper had called in. This was, of course, completely unfair; how could all the work get done by just one helper? I told him that it sounded like he needed to stop talking to me about it and start getting it done. He was shocked that I was so unfeeling to his problem and would have kept going, but my phone started to ring. I told him to "save it for Facebook" and answered the phone. He left, but of course complained about me to Diana. She told me later that she had a number of complaints about me, and I needed to be nicer and friendlier to everyone. I told her if that wasn't the pot calling the kettle black, I didn't know what was. She insisted that I was the mean one in the office, and I reminded her that she wasn't called the Dragon Lady for nothing. We agreed to disagree about which one of us was meaner. She did say that there were a number of employees who would only come to the office if I was not there. I didn't tell her about the growing number who only came to see me, terrified of asking her for help. I never refused to help anyone, whether I liked them or not. It was my job to answer questions and solve employee problems, and I tried to do it as best I could. I may not smile and be cheerful to some, but I did answer their questions.

There were plenty of characters in the store; a big store has a large employee base, and you are bound to have some a little weirder than others. One who the whole store knew was a young woman who seemed to bring her whole life with her each day. She would haul in two over-stuffed backpacks of personal items, making us wonder if she was homeless and just brought everything she owned with her each day. That wasn't what was really unusual; she had a love of music and believed she had a voice fit for Hollywood. The unusual bit was that she would sing very loudly for all to hear. Next to the pop machines outside the break room was a small alcove where employees could hang up coats and umbrellas. She claimed this area as her stage and would put on her headphones and sing at the top of her lungs into her hairbrush while "dancing" along. She was shorter and heavier than me, but it didn't stop her from twerking. She put on quite a show, oblivious to stares or laughter. We called her "Dancing Queen." She put on a loud and off-key performance daily, and no manager dared to try and stop her; any who interrupted her concert were subject to a verbal berating. I think management also saw it as a blessing; it kept employees from loitering around the break room. Her shows were certain to clear the hallway. The really annoying part was if she was in the middle of a "concert," she would not move so others could get their coats to leave. One quiet and shy woman was waiting but needed to get her coat and catch the bus. She saw me and asked for my help. I just elbowed past Dancing Queen, and she bumped against the wall. She was furious, but I sharply told her that she didn't own the corner; others needed to be able to get their things, and she needed to move out of their way. She stormed off, cursing and yelling. The crowd who had gathered gave me a grateful round of applause as they got their things to leave. When one of the managers saw me later, he told me that she came to complain about me. I told him that if he and the others had any balls, they would have handled the situation by now, and I wouldn't have had to do anything. He decided it wasn't worth the fight and just asked me to stay away from her. She got told that she could not block access to everyone's coats and such and afterward avoided me like the plague.

There was never a dull moment in HR. My interruptions were interrupted, and I became queen of the Post-It notes. I kept pads at my desk and would quickly jot notes when five things were happening at once (which was most of the time). I would be on the phone when some employee would need my help, and I could take down their name and problem quickly and then resolve it later. I was overjoyed when a friend gave me a huge pack for Christmas. Some days I would go through a whole stack in my shift, but they saved me time and again from forgetting tasks and important messages. Coworkers would leave me notes too; one young woman answered my office phone one day and left me a note "someone called about something." I thanked her and kindly asked her not to answer my phone again.

Another job of HR was assigning employee lockers for their personal items. There were a bunch of small lockers, twelve-inch cubes, big enough for a purse, light jacket, or lunchbox. A logbook was kept in HR, and I was responsible for assigning new hires a locker and cleaning out lockers of employees who had quit or gotten fired. Each locker had a combination lock, and I kept the codes in the book also. I often had to look up codes for people who had forgotten theirs and usually help new hires to open them. I tried to assign lockers based on height and age. The five-foot-tall woman could barely reach the top row lockers, let alone see inside to get her things in and out. And the man at retirement age probably didn't want to stoop to the floor for his locker on the bottom row. When someone left, I would empty their locker about a week later. My predecessor had not, and when I took over, I had to do a huge locker cleanup that took a month. But it didn't take long if I stayed up on it, which I tried to do. Some people cleaned out their locker when they left; others left everything. I found lockers filled with trash and old food, spilled drinks and chewed gum. I would empty and clean them out for the next person and then go on to the next locker.

One I went to clean had something crusted all over the inside, down the front, and into the locker below. I was scrubbing it and wondering what it could be when the employee with the locker next to it came in. She asked what I was doing, and I told her that person had quit, and I was trying to clean up the mess they had made in their locker and trying to figure out what it was. She told me that the owner was sick last week and had thrown up while removing something from her locker. The owner ran to the bathroom and didn't come back. I was glad the mystery was solved, not so glad to be cleaning up someone's vomit. I finished, went and scrubbed my hands, and used a large amount of hand sanitizer from Diana's desk. She was a big germophobe; if I cleared my throat, she insisted I was getting a cold and would spray me with disinfectant. While rubbing in the hand sanitizer, her phone rang, so I answered it. She came in just as I was hanging up and asked what I had been doing. When I told her I had cleaned up vomit just before answering her phone, she went crazy, spraying her whole desk with disinfectant and wiping her phone with bleach wipes. I just laughed and laughed. No matter how many times I told her that I had thoroughly washed my hands, she kept scrubbing and cleaning her desk.

Diana also held me personally responsible if anything was missing off her desk. She left the office often to talk to the manager about problems or concerns, and I was to watchdog her desk and supplies while she was gone. God help anyone caught taking so much as a paper clip; she was very possessive of her office supplies. I asked her if she was taught to share in kindergarten as I was; she told me the teacher had tried and failed. I believed her. She was very stingy with rubber bands, paper clips, Post-Its, and pens. She directed everyone needing those to my desk; I was to share with the world all that I had. I bought supplies at back-to-school sales and would bring in bags of cheap pens and such and keep them in my locked file cabinet, bringing out a few at a time. We each had a locked file cabinet for our personal items, and all other cabinets in the room were kept locked at all times. Everything in HR is confidential and must be kept locked away to protect privacy. When we left for the day, we would lock up our desk items or the next morning they would be gone. Once we left, any manager on duty would come into our office and try to hide from everyone. They would also look for pens and such to steal for their office. Staplers were a hot item; the managers broke theirs all the time and would come to use ours. Diana had a very nice one she had bought. One manager loved to sneak in while she was busy or in the bathroom and steal it, just to listen to her yell and storm down the hall, demanding it back. She would retrieve it and then yell at me for allowing it to be taken. I suggested she bolt it to her desk, but she did not think that was funny. I suggested it to the thief; he found that idea very funny but did not do it. He knew better than to press his luck with Diana.

You have to get used to being interrupted in retail. I don't just mean when you are talking, but while doing anything. No matter what task you are working on, when a customer comes with a question, you must stop and help them and then be able to pick up where you left off. HR was this times ten, I don't think I ever completed a task start to finish without at least one interruption, and more often five. Retail is always a juggling act of many things happening at once, but some days it was ridiculous. Too many times, I would be on the phone while working on the computer, then while on hold, an employee would need help. Then I would hear the printer beeping because it was out of paper; then the other phone would start to ring. Speakerphone was a godsend. I'd put the hold music on speaker while fixing the printer and answering the employee and other phone, then jump back to my call when someone finally picked up. Many employees would watch amazed as Diana and I did this dance daily. They would say that they could never do it; they would be overwhelmed and have a nervous breakdown. I usually didn't find it too hard; it's just learning how to prioritize and stay focused through the chaos.

There is always good and bad in any job. I enjoyed being off my feet and in a cool office instead of walking the store and sweating. And I liked the work; it was interesting and challenging. The main thing I disliked was being a babysitter; having to listen to everyone's complaints and problems and whining. I've never had much patience for that, maybe because I'm the youngest child or maybe because I was taught that complaining doesn't accomplish anything. You may not be happy about a situation, but you might as well get to work and get it done as soon as you can, so you can move on. I didn't like the idea of staying in HR forever; I knew one day I would snap at someone and really hurt some feelings. So, when another store was opening within ten blocks of my house, I decided to transfer. I loved the idea of being so close to home. I could come home for lunch, and it would save me hundreds a year on gas. It wasn't a hard decision to leave, but I had been at this particular store for twenty years. As I set my last day and got my transfer in order, I was surprised that Diana seemed sad to see me go. She did not often show much sentiment, but I believed she had enjoyed having me in the office. I was sad to leave a number of good friends and many memories behind. I had seen more changes and people come and go than I could count over the years. I had learned about every area of a retail store and had also learned a lot about how to work with different personalities and had indeed learned a lot about myself. On my last day, the employees gathered to say good-bye to me and two others also leaving. One was quitting retail, and the other was a manager on loan who was being promoted to another store. As everyone wished us well, we were asked to say a few words. I really don't remember what I said; I was surprised that I felt choked up at leaving. A large cake was brought out to celebrate us, I looked down to see it said "Good luck, Brian" for the manager who was leaving. *How nice to be acknowledged*, I thought to myself. Then Diana came and asked me to cut and serve the cake to everyone. So much for sentiment.

13

There was some discussion about what area I would take over at the new store. I had plenty of experience, so I had my choice. Although I wanted to stay off my feet, I did not want to take on HR at a brand-new store with brand-new employees. Not many others were going to transfer, so almost all the employees would be fresh off the street, not a task I wished to take on. But there are very few office jobs in retail stores, and the one area I really wanted was being eliminated in this new test store. I had hoped to take over the invoicing office, but it was being combined with claims, so I decided to become the claims manager. It was a pay raise and meant I could be off my feet at least part of the time. Also added to the claims manager was being in charge of store receiving and shipping. So, I was over everything that entered or left the back doors, everything that was broken or damaged in the store, and the paperwork that goes with it all. The receiving was the only thing I had not done before, and it was easy to learn. I went into the new store with full confidence the first day employees were allowed in. I guess it was a good thing I had confidence in myself; I quickly had none in my new managers. I remember coming home the first day and wondering what mess I had gotten myself into now.

In all my years, I had never opened a new store before. I was used to a kind of controlled-chaos workplace, but this was completely uncontrolled. The day we were allowed to take possession of the building, it was completely empty inside, just a hollow shell. Only the computers and phones were installed, and the phones didn't work. We had six weeks till the grand opening to build, set, and fill the whole store. Yikes. When I tried to get on a computer, I found that I had no options; those do not transfer from store to store.

I tracked down Gary the store manager, a man in his mid-forties who looked like he was having a panic attack. I almost asked him if he needed to breathe into a paper bag, but since there weren't any paper bags around, I didn't bother. If he didn't have high blood pressure before, I'm sure he had it now. I told Gary my problem of needing computer options, but he had no idea how to fix it. I told him I'd fix it if he would just sign on to a computer for just a minute. He agreed and stood by nervously. I wasn't worried about him watching what I was about to do since he obviously had no clue what I was doing. I quickly went to the menu to assign options and gave myself the ability to assign options to others. I signed him off the computer and thanked him for his help. He just looked confused and left, which was fine, since I no longer needed him. I signed myself on the computer and opened the menu to assign options, put in my name, and gave myself any options I thought I would need. It was a very useful trick I had learned years ago, and I still use it from time to time. All the new managers found out that I knew how to assign options, and since none of them knew how to do it, they sent all the new hires to me. It is something only managers are supposed to do, but that has never stopped me before. I spent my whole first day setting up computer equipment and assigning options to employees and managers.

The second day, the real "fun" started. I was given a set of keys to the receiving dock and a walkie-talkie. An hour into my shift, semis started rolling in, full of warehouse steel shelving, grid shelving, upright beams, display racks, sales floor shelving, and cash registers. I spent the day directing traffic in and out of the bays and around the back of the store, unloading those trucks as fast as I could, so the next ones could dock and unload. I would call on the radio what had just been unloaded, so the correct crew knew to come back and get their pieces to be set up on the sales floor. Jerry was our IT guru from the home office, a really nice guy who was a whiz at setting up registers, computers, and printers for the store. He also was the boss in charge of the layout and setup of all fixtures. He and I exchanged cell numbers since way too many people had radios and liked to talk on them way too much. If I couldn't get him on the radio, I would just call his cell and let him know what had been delivered so he could make sure it went to the correct area. I was constantly being called; my name was said so much on that radio, I swore I was going to change it. All day I was called as crews tried to find the fixtures they needed. Many pieces came separately, sometimes on different trucks and even different days.

An employee was sent from another store to help me at the door. She had experience at the door and immediately began bossing me. She very vocal about what was wrong with our store. Nothing was set up as it was in her store, and therefore my store was completely wrong. She had a fit about how dark the back room was; we had skylights, and the store lights would automatically dim if it was sunny out. She felt my desk area was too dark and I needed some kind of light over it. She also insisted I get a clipboard to hold any paperwork, a stapler, paper clips, pens, and a file cabinet to keep supplies in. She carried on for two hours about how she could never work in these conditions, until I'd had enough. I informed her that since no actual merchandise had been delivered yet, I had no way to get a file cabinet, stapler, pens, paper clips, or even a clipboard. I very sharply told her that I was doing the best I could with what I had. She decided it was too stressful for her and went back to her own store. I wasn't trying to be mean, but her complaining was not helping me in any way, and I'd rather work alone than listen to it. For three weeks, I controlled the back door alone, then the next three weeks the merchandise started to flow in. I was finally sent help to train to work with me after the store was opened.

The first one was a young man who seemed bright enough but was more interested in girls than work. Romo did learn quickly and did all right without much babysitting, but if I didn't keep an eye on him, he would start to chase all the new young girls around, trying to collect phone numbers and make plans for dates. He quickly started to work his way through the female workforce and got quite a reputation. A couple of girls tried to hang on to him, but he was only interested in an easy hookup. I didn't care what he did at home; I just needed him to stay on track at work. Romo did a good enough job, and I started leaving him in charge of the back door while I trained my second person at the claims area. The claims area was also to be a secured area for file storage, resulting in a large metal grid cage with shelves inside for file boxes and a long desk for two computers and a phone and outside shelves to hold damaged items while we worked to process them.

The second helper was very quiet, and although she said she understood something after I explained it, it became clear very quickly that she had understood nothing. Susie also worked very slowly, earning her the nickname "the snail." She did as little as possible; when we were supposed to be working together, she would stand back and let me do everything, claiming she was trying not to get in my way. I would try to leave her to do the work, but if she was not supervised, then she would go sit in the cage and try to hide behind boxes and pretend to work while playing on her phone. She soon found that I made frequent trips from the door to the cage and would catch her goofing off, so she would work as slowly as possible till my shift ended and then would hide in the cage after I left for the rest of her shift. I guess it was a good thing she didn't do much, because most of what she did was wrong and had to be redone. Careless help is usually worse than no help at all.

The place was a tornado of activity, with employees and managers hurrying from one task to the next. Each area had to be set with aisles built from the ground up. Eight-foot-tall "T" pieces are linked together with bracers. Pegboard slides down the channels between, and a top bar holds them in place. Base decks are next, and then shelves are snapped in place at the correct heights, per home office modular. Endcaps are attached to each end for displays. An experienced crew of four can build an aisle start to finish in less than thirty minutes. It's actually a lot easier with no more than four. More people just get in the way, and you spend more time trying not to hit each other with the pieces. There were also clothing racks and tables to be built. And certain areas have special lock-up displays to be assembled. I had immediately told everyone that any assembly must be done on the floor. I was responsible for the back room, and I intended to keep it organized.

Three weeks out, the sales floor was set. Now we just needed products to fill the shelves. Semis started arriving full of dry goods, clothing, home goods, toys, and such. Chaos continued as managers discovered that many areas were not set properly. Shelves were at the wrong heights, sections that were supposed to have pegs did not, tables and racks were switched everywhere. Gary wanted me to help reset the sales floor, but quickly found out that without me, the back room flow stopped. Employees from the other stores in town came, some to help and some, it seemed, just to argue. Two almost came to blows about how to set the food modulars. One insisted that to set shelves, you count from the bottom shelf slot, half covered by the base deck. The other said you start with the first completely visible slot. I was called to give my expert opinion, since of all the people in the building, I had been with the company the longest. I announced to everyone that the proper way was to start with the first completely visible slot and count up to the proper height for each shelf. The loser stormed out of the store, swearing that we would all look like idiots at the grand opening. The winner and I shook our heads and got back to work.

I sent Suzie out to help fill shelves; until products came in, we basically had no claims to do, and she had proven useless at the back door, quickly getting overwhelmed and unable to keep up or unload a truck without help. Other stores would send us extra products to help fill the sales floor. Those items had to be counted for accuracy and then checked into our computer system. It is not that difficult a process; the items come with a printout, and you match that with what was sent. Romo was good help in this; he was fast and accurate. Susie was not, unable to even verify contents, let alone enter items into the computer. I doubted she would ever learn the job, but right then I was just trying to get ready for the grand opening.

My third helper came in the day before our grand opening. I was being pulled in every direction and had no time for her that day, so I sent her to continue her computer quizzes and stay out of my hair. I wasn't trying to be mean; I just had no time at that moment for another person constantly asking me questions. The place was going crazy; you could almost feel the whole building shaking. I was sure the store manager was going to have a stroke before it was over. I was also sure he wasn't going to last six months with us. He seemed to have no backbone, and definitely no clue. There were a ton of visiting bigwigs and managers from other stores trying to make sure we were ready to open. They took charge and gave orders while Gary followed behind. The back door had finally calmed down, all the deliveries had been made, and now the shelves just needed to be filled and the final clean and polish done.

When I came in the next morning, we looked like a real store, ready for business. I walked through the store, feeling very proud. We had taken an empty building and made a retail store open for business in just six weeks. It was quite an experience. I had been through many store remodels, but at least now we didn't have to work and watch for customers at the same time. For that fact, prepping for opening was easier, but it was not something I wished to do again.

At 9 a.m., a big ceremony was planned for the grand opening with a speech or two, pictures, cake, and punch. I stayed in the back; I had plenty of work to do and was quite sure I didn't want to listen to any speeches. Besides, I now had to start training my third crew member. She seemed nice and willing to learn, listening and asking questions about what we were doing and why. I thought she would be a big improvement over Suzie, who never asked anything, just nodded as if she understood. She seemed like she would be okay for the first month. Romo was doing well, and my only weak link was Suzie. Or so I thought.

14

I tried to get us settled into a routine. Romo would come in for the 5 a.m. shift and work till 2 p.m. I would work 7 a.m. to 4 p.m., and Suzie and my new teammate worked 9 a.m. to 6 p.m. This worked well for a bit, but then trouble started. Romo not only had a weakness for the ladies; he also had a weakness for beer. He would call in to work because he was hung over, leaving no one to cover the door till I showed up two hours later. Management got very tired of this, so did the vendors and drivers who needed to be waited on. At first it was sporadic, but soon was at least once a week, then twice, then sometimes three times. So, my shift was quickly changed to come in at 5 a.m. also, just to make sure someone was there to cover the door. This left the girls alone for almost half their shift, and the lack of supervision showed. Add the fact that we were entering the holiday season with a very green crew, and I started staying late each day to help get things done and solve problems.

I also got asked to help on Saturdays. Suzie was supposed to work the weekends, but it was too much for her to cover claims and the door. It should not have been that difficult, but she was too slow and was completely unable to find and fix any mistake she made while checking in vendors. I got tired of being called at home to come in and help her, so

I just started working on Saturdays and racked up the overtime. I was scheduled forty hours a week, but for the first six months we were open, I worked fifty to fifty-five hours each week. My feet didn't thank me, but I did like the paychecks.

The same time Romo started to miss work, my third team member started to change. Cece had seemed fine in the beginning; now she started to miss work too, and when she did come in, you could never guess her mood. Anything could set her off; sometimes she would have a screaming tirade, and other times she would just walk out and go home without a word to anyone. One employee walked past her to go to the break room, and Cece said hello, but the other girl didn't hear her and did not respond. This caused a huge meltdown. She went to the manager to file a complaint against the girl, insisting that she hated her and was spreading gossip about her, trying to get her fired. That incident earned her the nickname "Crazy" throughout the store, and most employees tried to avoid her after that. She started spreading rumors about myself, Romo, and Suzie around the store and would go all day without speaking to any of us. Romo just ignored her; when he did show up, he covered the door and stayed as far away from her as he could. Suzie just said nothing. As long as she did not argue or put up any fight, Cece left her alone. That meant that she directed all her craziness at me.

I guess I'll never know why she started behaving as she did, but it was a real rollercoaster working with her. Despite all I had learned over the years about working with different people and different personalities, nothing helped when trying to deal with her. Her attendance became more unpredictable. She would either not come in or come in two hours late, but you could bet she surely would not come in on time. One day she, Romo, and I were all scheduled to work, but of course, Romo called in again, so I was left to cover the door and claims alone. I tried to get done what I could in claims, since she was so unreliable. Sure enough, she did not come in on time, but finally showed up two and a half hours late. Of course, she had not called that she would be late; that would be an adult thing to do, and she acted more and more like an out-of-control two-year-old each day. When she finally showed up, I commented how nice it was that she finally bothered to come to work. She got upset and stormed off to hide in the bathroom for thirty minutes before leaving work and heading back home. Unfortunately, this became the norm, not the exception. During all this, Suzie got a free pass. I had no time for her while trying to deal with my two ghosts. That was Suzie's only positive trait: she showed up every day on time, eager to collect her paycheck while doing no work. Sad to say, she was the least of my problems.

We had pulled off the grand opening and were now up and running. This should have been settling into a routine of unloading trucks, getting the freight to the floor, and waiting on customers. But our green management team was quickly lost in the weeds. Gary seemed incapable of leading them, and employee turnover was starting to skyrocket. Those few of us with experience were being run ragged. I wasn't the only one working twelve-hour days, six days a week. The stress was already taking its toll, and we had not been open six months. Nothing good was happening at our store; Gary and his completely ineffective management team were running us into the ground.

You never know what might happen when you show up for work. But I can tell you with certainty that no two days will be the same. And when you least expect it, a situation will arise that you have never seen before. When you reach five years of employment, home office sends the store a certificate with your name and years stamped in gold, thanking you for your service. I had received one every five years, and they were supposed to be given at a store meeting so everyone could clap for you and shake their heads in disbelief that anyone could stay so long. Sometimes mine were given at a meeting; other times the certificate was just handed to me with a pat on the back and a "get back to work." I didn't care anymore; I did not need the store to recognize my years. But this year was special—it was my twenty-five-year anniversary. Gary decided that he needed to make a big deal about it. Since this was the most positive thing happening, he decided it needed a celebration. He had the bakery make up a big cake, nicely decorated, proclaiming my name and thanks for twenty-five years. He called all the employees to the back door where I was, for a special meeting to congratulate me. Everyone showed up at the back door and gathered around where I was working. I looked around, very confused, wondering why all these employees were back in my work area. Gary brought me forward and began making some speech about how great it was that I had been with the company for twenty-five years and how much I was appreciated because of all my knowledge and experience. He shook my hand, and everyone clapped as he gave me my certificate and even a plaque, engraved with my name. I then realized what was happening but was powerless to stop it.

It's not that I didn't appreciate what everyone was doing; there was only one problem. Those certificates are sent to the store two months early, so any recognition could be planned properly. Gary did not know that, and obviously had not really looked at the certificate. It clearly says the employee's name, years of service, and *month* of hire. He orchestrated this very nice party in February, not April when I was actually hired. I could do nothing now but go along with it and smile and spend the day thanking everyone for their well wishes. And in April, when my actual anniversary date rolled around, it was read off at the morning meeting along with sales numbers and any birthdays. Then I had another parade of people, now sounding disgusted with me (like I wanted more recognition), because my anniversary had already been celebrated, and I clearly wanted more credit than I deserved. I tried to explain to the first couple who made comments, but I finally just told people that it was a paperwork snafu so they would stop giving me the evil eye. Thankfully, it all blew over quickly.

I had dealt with the unreliable Romo till after the holidays; now he was moved off my team to work an evening shift. Management hoped he would come to work more if he wasn't expected to be up by 5 a.m. Hopefully he had slept off his hangover by the time his new shift started at 4 p.m. He hated it and came crying to me that he wanted to come back to my team. He just knew I wanted him back, as he had done a good job at the door. I explained that the best help in the world does me no good passed out on his floor at home. He kept at me, but I refused to take him back. I was not surprised when he quit a month later.

15

I was desperate for some decent help, and an angel came to my rescue. I had worked with him before at the other store. I was in HR when he was hired, and so we knew each other. I also knew he was very intelligent, hard-working, and motivated to be promoted. Charles was a flamboyant gay man who could act like a real diva, but I thought he was hilarious. We had always gotten along, but he told me he was a little nervous to work directly with me. I asked why, and he said he knew that I went to church and hoped his being gay would not affect how I treated him. I told him that right now I didn't care if he was purple with horns growing out of his head; I just needed good help. We never had a problem working together; I finally was able to laugh and relax just a bit with him there. Of course, he and Cece butted heads immediately, but I loved that he was able to say things to her that I could not.

She had already filed numerous complaints about me mistreating her, so I was told to be very careful what I said. But when she tried to file a complaint about Charles, he filed a counter complaint that she was homophobic. They were both told to try not to speak to each other, but that was never going to happen. Charles learned quickly, and to try to keep them apart, I would send him to the door if she showed up, and

I would try to work with her. There wasn't much work going on; you can't work effectively and cause ten kinds of drama at the same time. I was still working the early shift; Charles wasn't a morning person and hated to come in at five. So, I had him take the 7 a.m. shift; at least I knew he would come in and get things rolling before Suzie showed up to do nothing and Cece decided whether to put in an appearance or not. I asked Charles to work with Suzie and see if he could get her to learn anything or at least make an effort, but he quickly declared her useless and gave up. I guess it wasn't a bad thing that she did so little work. Anything she did do was wrong and had to be redone. I'd rather correct her little bit than a whole day's work.

About once a month, Cece would get the idea that she needed to clean up the claims area and would process out anything she found. I had to spend the next couple of days finding and fixing everything she had done wrong.

I was constantly badgering management to get rid of her, but they resisted, insisting that then I would be short-handed. I'll never understand why management thinks that crap help is better than no help. All crap help does is bring down the morale of everyone who has to pull the extra weight for the lazy person. It's hard to keep a strong work ethic when the person next to you is paid the same amount while you do the work for both of you. I just don't get why management keeps worthless people around. The only one benefiting is the one getting paid for not working. Cece caused me way more work and stress when she was there; I would have been overjoyed to see her gone. But I found out that she had filed complaints about every supervisor and manager in the store, so the orders from home office were to bide time and build a case before she could be fired. I figured it wouldn't take long with all her nonsense, but it took way longer than I ever dreamed.

The number-one reason people get fired from retail is for attendance. It's the easiest thing to prove; you can't argue that it is unfair when you really didn't show up for work again and again. It's much harder to make a case for unprofessional behavior, being unproductive, or causing problems with other employees. It's easy to see it happening but hard to prove when your subject will claim a thousand excuses why none of that is their fault or someone has a grudge against them. But we all make the choice to show up each day we are scheduled, so when you choose not to come, there isn't much of an argument you can make. So, you might think that she'd have been gone in just a month, with as much work as she missed, but the other side is that management must track her attendance and count all the time missed as unexcused. That is the piece that never happened. I couldn't do it myself; it had to be done by a salaried manager, and attendance tracking is usually pretty low on their priority list. Especially in a new store with all these green employees and just-as-green managers. Gary was missing in action, and most of the others had already figured out all about Cece and just tried to keep their distance. Plus, they were unwilling to put their necks on the line to fire her, since she had so many complaints filed with home office. I had to deal with her as best I could, constantly praying she would just stop showing up completely. Unfortunately, I'm not that lucky.

The stunts she pulled left me shaking my head in disbelief. One day after I had to leave early for an appointment, Cece and Suzie were left there by themselves. I knew perfectly well that no work was going to get done, but the next day, I heard all about what Cece did do. Our HR was a guy I knew from the other store. He was very nice and came to me often with questions or just to vent about how insane his job was. He came to me the next day and asked me if I had enjoyed meeting Cece's dog. I asked him what on earth he was talking about; he said that the day before, she had brought her dog into the back room and was introducing him to everyone. I told him that I had left early and had not gotten to meet her dog but thanked him for letting me know. When she did show up that day for work, I took her aside and asked her to tell me about her dog. She tried to act like she had no idea what I was talking about, but I had heard it from other employees, not just HR, and had our security team verify it by watching the videos from the day before.

"Tell me about your dog," I said, as calmly as I could.

"I don't know what you mean," she said, lying to my face.

"Why was your dog in this store?" I asked, staring at her.

She decided that being snotty was her best approach. "I didn't know dogs weren't allowed in the store. I see customers with their dogs in here all the time."

I answered her firmly. "Service dogs are allowed in with customers. You are not a customer, and your dog is not allowed in this back room. Why did you have it back here?"

"I never had him in the back room." Another lie.

My irritation was building. "That is not what a number of employees have told me. They said you had him back here and were introducing him to everyone in the break room. Do you realize that there are cameras all around this store, including this back room, and the whole incident has been recorded? Are you going to tell me the truth, or should we continue this conversation in the managers' office?"

Now that she was caught in her lies, you might think she would change her tone. She didn't. "Oh. Well, my dog groomer had to close early for a family emergency and called to ask if I could pick up my dog. I told her I was at work. Could she just bring him by here? She pulled up out back, and I let him in the back door. Then I took him out the front door and took him home." She acted as if all this was a normal occurrence.

"So you-"received"-your dog at our back receiving door, paraded him around to every employee you could find, then finally walked him through the store out the front door to put him in your car and take him home. And none of this seemed like a ridiculous thing to do?" My temper blew, and I struggled to keep from yelling at her. I wouldn't have been so angry if she hadn't tried to lie about it and then act like it wasn't a big deal. Obviously, she wasn't as concerned about back room protocols as I was.

Suddenly, she was hysterical. "Just what exactly should I have done? You tell me, since you know everything!"

I lost it and let myself yell at her. "How about tell you groomer to meet you at your car, and then take him home instead of bringing him in the store at all? I guess that never crossed your mind. Why the hell would you think it is fine to bring your dog in here? Do we have national bring-your-pet-to-work days? What in God's name is wrong with you?"

At this point, she stormed off; I think she planned to file another complaint but thought better of it while hiding in the bathroom again. Perhaps she realized that she was in the wrong about the dog, and making a case of how I yelled her would only add fuel to the fire she was standing in. Once again, she hid for a while and then came back to claims to get her coat and leave for the day without a word to anyone. My stress levels and blood pressure were rising daily.

16

As I had predicted, Gary was transferred out after just six months at the store. That was pretty unheard of; usually a manager is left at the store at least a year before being pulled. But we were the *Titanic* and sinking fast. Our replacement was a manager with experience, but I didn't have much hope, as he was similar to Gary, but calmer. He didn't run around like he was about to have a heart attack, but he had no backbone either. Donny might have done well in his last store (a small hometown location), but I was sure he also wouldn't last here. This store needed a strong leader who would not let the employees run the place. I predicted six months again before another change would have to be made.

Donny was at least friendly; he would stop and chat with everyone, whereas Gary would hide in his office, terrified to look any of us in the face. But being too friendly is not effective either. You spend all day listening to people tell you how hard their job is and what you should do to make it easier (usually get more help so the pressure is off them to get anything done). A thousand problems were staring him in the face, but Donny seemed only concerned with how the store looked. He was obsessed with the parking lot; it constantly needed to be swept, cigarette butts and trash picked up, and the front doors cleaned and polished. He came back and asked me to sweep up trash out behind the store. I just gave him a look but didn't argue. There is a team for cleaning the store, but apparently, he had them busy cleaning other areas. I just shrugged and took care of it, wondering if he knew that cleanliness may be next to godliness, but it is not next to sales goals. He was either oblivious to the problems or so overwhelmed by them that he was paralyzed and could not see how to solve them. His management team was completely ineffective; turnover was astronomical, training was nonexistent, etc. All over the store, there were empty shelves, empty displays, and mislabeled products, but his daily notes were to sweep here, clean there, and pick up things everywhere. Most of the supervisors or leads were drowning, those without experience having no clue what to do, those with experience having no backup to do what needed to be done. We were in a desperate situation, and if something didn't change quickly, I feared the store would be closed before we really got a chance to get going.

While switching out store managers, most of the rest of the management team was changed too. Some of our green team was moved to other stores, and more experienced managers were brought in. It gave me just a bit of hope; at least this group had some problem-solving skills, and of course, I knew most of them from my years working at the other store. That store had been a training store, so almost all of them had spent some time there. This store was a test store; new programs were tried here so the bugs could be worked out before being implemented elsewhere. That sounds like a good plan: have the brand-new store test brand-new programs, but only a fool would think you can test things with a green team, not a dream team. As weeks passed, this new group of managers worked hard to bring the store back. The downward spiral was perhaps not stopped but slowed dramatically. That was something, at least.

Since the new managers and I already knew each other, they trusted that I was holding my area together and let me be. They quickly learned all about Cece and her truckload of problems, but they were too busy trying to put out fires everywhere else in the store to deal with her. It was on the list of problems to solve, but I'd have to wait my turn. But a reprieve came. Cece requested a leave of absence, which was quickly approved, and I got three months of relief from her madness.

While she was out, the Suzie problem solved itself. One day she didn't show up for work; in fact, she never came back. I never knew why, but I figured she got a different job doing nothing. I sure wasn't sorry, but now Charles and I were really being run ragged trying to do everything ourselves. I demanded more help, which probably would have been ignored, except we had a compliance visit, and claims was a real mess, and many violations were noted. I spoke to the compliance officer and explained that I was short two people very suddenly. With his recommendation, I was assigned another helper. She had been a lead over a number of areas of the store but had gotten really stressed out and wanted a break. She had let the manager know he could either move her or lose her, meaning she was ready to quit if he didn't let her change areas, so she ended up with me.

Lani was a small woman but full of fire, a real firecracker. *Dynamite* was an apt description, a big bang in a small package. I felt like I had hit the jackpot; Lani and Charles were both great help—smart, willing to learn, and hard-working. We had three months of really being able to enjoy coming to work (a rarity in retail). The three of us joked and laughed together as I taught them all the aspects of our jobs. Charles kept us laughing daily. Our intercom sound system was messed up, and to play music in the store, home office sent a CD that was replayed continually. We listened to the same CD of current pop hits for eight months straight until we had the whole miserable playlist memorized. I was not familiar with most of the songs and quickly hated all of them. Charles would loudly sing to his favorites and just as loudly complain about the ones he hated, critiquing the lyrics, tempo, chorus, whatever. We were all sick to death of hearing the same eighteen crappy songs day in and day out, but his jokes made them more bearable. That's the great thing about working with friends: they help pass the time on mundane days and still make you laugh on the most stressful days. My days were so much easier with the two of them. I no longer was working fifteen hours of overtime each week and was able to feel like I was actually accomplishing something at work. I finally had a team working together.

But all good things must come to an end sometime, and mine ended when Cece came back from her leave. Her arrival back was just as sudden as her departure, and it took only five minutes for the drama to start again. Lani, Charles, and I were all working near the claims cage when she waltzed in. She walked up to me, looked me in the eye, and said hello like she'd never been gone. I said hello back and continued to work, entering the claims cage to get a report I needed. Charles and Lani were in the cage, watching to see what she was going to do. She followed me in and then started yelling at me, saying she was tired of me being mean to her and treating her like shit. She'd had enough of it and wouldn't take it anymore. I told her that I didn't realize saying hello was treating her badly. She continued to yell and curse at me about how I was such a terrible person that everyone hated, blah blah blah. Lani left the room and headed straight for the managers' office to report what had happened. After a bit, she came back and told Cece she was to go to the office; the manager wanted to speak to her. I was called down after about thirty minutes to give my version of what had happened. I relayed my story as Cece sat there looking furious. I also noted how peaceful and calm it had been while she was gone, and how it only took her a few minutes to start drama and bring work to a standstill. She was told to go get caught up on her computer quizzes for the rest of the day and stay away from the claims area while the manager tried to find a resolution. I went back to claims and found that Charles had gone to cover the door while Lani caught me to tell me what she had said to the manager.

We were quietly speaking about it when suddenly I looked and saw Cece, standing outside the cage wall, pressing her face to the grid, trying to listen in. It was like something out of a horror movie, when you think you are safe, but the deranged maniac is just outside, waiting for you. I told her I thought she was supposed to be doing her computer quizzes, not hanging around the claims cage, and she stomped off and left for the day. She missed the next two days, and I thought maybe this was it and she'd never come back. But she did come back and continued her old tricks: coming in late, not coming in at all, spreading gossip, and just generally causing drama wherever she went.

After her talking-to, she decided to change tactics with me. Instead of huge screaming outbursts, now she quietly went about backstabbing and undermining me. She would go around the store and tell any random supervisor or area lead that I had talked badly about them. Some believed it and tried to file complaints against me; some knew better and came and told me what she was doing. I had many hours wasted being called to the office to explain myself about the complaints. As soon as management found out that Cece was at the heart of it, everything was dropped, and I could get back to work. She kept at it, but soon the whole store knew better than to believe anything she said. She didn't try much with Lani, and she had already tried and failed with Charles. I was her primary target, and she took aim at me daily. She continued to make plenty of mistakes, though I think most were on purpose, just so I'd have to waste time checking everything she did and fixing it. I took pictures and documented all I could to keep making a case against her.

At least I now had an ally; a new supervisor came in over me and my team. I had never worked with him but quickly found out that he was a stickler for accuracy. I showed him my file of mistakes she had made, and he promised to work to get her out of my area. If he could not get her fired, at least he could get her moved, and she would no longer be my problem.

One of her tricks was familiar. Anytime I was on the phone, she would come near and mutter rude comments and curse at me. The first time she did it, I was completely annoyed. The second time, a light went off, and I remembered Blondie doing this same thing many years before. I also remembered that Blondie often talked of her daughter, a woman who should be about my age. I called my best friend Vee that night and asked her about it. She did remember Blondie talking about her daughter, and when I said Cece's name, she gasped. She agreed it was the same name, and the age would be about right too. She thought it was unbelievable that I was reliving an old nightmare; I had to be wrong. But I was sure I was right; there were too many similarities to be a coincidence.

How nice to see that the apple had not fallen far from the tree. I did feel like I had a bit of the upper hand now. I certainly knew what behaviors to watch for and knew my best defense was to take the high road and never stoop to her level. It was the only way; I could never match her skills at lying or backstabbing. The next day, after she did the phone trick, I calmly mentioned that I used to work with a woman who did the same thing. As I described Blondie and used her true name, Cece's eyes got big, and she suddenly turned and left the room. I took that as confirmation I was correct—this was indeed Blondie's daughter. She did keep at me daily, but I think she knew her days were numbered.

She also went to work on Lani and Charles. She spread gossip about Lani talking about others, but management had learned to ignore it. She orchestrated things, and through lies and manipulation, did manage to get Charles fired. He tried to fight it, and I did all I could to help him, but I lost him from the team. It sucked, and she crowed about her victory all through the store. Lani and I were furious; it took all I could do to keep Lani calm and not cuss or punch Cece out. I sure couldn't afford to lose Lani, and she knew if she did anything, Cece would press to get her fired too. Lani wasn't about to give Cece the satisfaction. It was tough, but the noose around Cece was closing in.

Finally, things were about to break my way, and then Donny caved to Cece and refused to fire her. I insisted that he move her, but he said he had to wait till a replacement was hired. I was done waiting and did something I had never done in twenty-five years with the company. I emailed the state HR officer and told him the whole story. I knew him from my time in HR; I didn't care much for him, but I did know him, and he knew me. He did investigate the situation, even came into the store to interview Donny, other managers who had dealt with Cece, and me. I went over all my documents, had him pull up her attendance record, and outlined what had been happening and how long I had dealt with it and how many times I had begged management to do something about the situation. He was my last resort; all my hope was on him. He promised to continue his investigation and come to a decision by the end of the week. When I left the office, he called Donny back in, looking and sounding quite displeased with this whole situation. I felt a spark of hope that maybe this would all end soon. As soon as Cece heard she was wanted in the office, she took off and left the store. I was glad; I suppose she thought she was dodging a bullet, but it was actually another nail in her coffin. Two days later, when she came back to work, I was called to the office and told she was going to be fired. I was to go back to claims and not speak to her, as a manager came and took her to the office to fill out the paperwork to let her go. I did exactly as I was told (for once), not wanting to risk anything stopping this from happening.

After she was led to the office, another manager came to claims and sat and started working at one of the computers. He said nothing to me, just kept working. I asked no questions, just picked up where she had been working and got busy. It wasn't unusual for any manager to use our computers, but after he stayed more than fifteen minutes, I knew something was up. I guessed he was there to make sure that when they were done with her in the office, she didn't come back and try to start more trouble. I was fine with that; he and I just kept working in silence. Lani came from the door and asked what was going on. I just shook my head at her, and she got the hint. She went to lunch, and about an hour after he came in, he got a call and then left without a word. I guessed that meant that it was done, and she had left the building. As soon as he left, I darted to the computer and pulled up one of my old HR screens that shows employee status. I put in her name, and sure enough, it showed fired. After being promised this would happen for months, I finally could see it in black and white. I took a picture of the screen before I signed off, a giant weight lifted off me. After 361 days, I was finally done with Cece. It was the last act of Donny; he was reassigned to another store after just five months. Again, my prediction proved correct. Now if only I could predict lottery numbers with such accuracy!

17

Lani and I celebrated, so glad to be done with the drama. It had been beyond stressful trying to keep the work going with just the two of us. The next step was to get the team built back up, and a new person was moved within a week. I wasn't given any options about who was chosen; it didn't really matter, as no one could be as bad as Cece. This woman had been working in the accounting office, but that job was being changed, and there were no longer hours for her. I didn't know much about her, but Lil was nice the few times I had talked to her. The first day she was to train in claims, I smelled her before I saw her. She had apparently poured an entire bottle of perfume on herself right before she came to work. It was a cloud that enveloped her, so strong I could taste it. I am rather sensitive to chemical smells; they give me a terrible headache in just minutes. I'd rather smell someone's body odor than too much perfume. I grew up on a farm and had smelled my share of manure. Before we could even begin training, I had a headache, which I knew would be a migraine by the end of the day. There was no way I could work in her cloud; I'd have to do something immediately.

"I'm not trying to hurt your feelings," I told her, "but I am very sensitive to strong smells, and your perfume is giving me a headache. I'm sure it smells nice; it's just too strong for me. I need you not to wear it while you work back here," I said.

"Oh, does it bother you?" she asked. Even though I had just said that, I still tried to be nice. After all, it was her first day in claims.

"Yes, it really does bother me. I'm not trying to be mean or say you don't smell good; it is just way too strong for me. Please do not wear it while you work with me," I said, hoping I was being clear.

"Oh, well, okay," she said. "If you don't like my perfume, then I guess I won't wear it around you," she said, her feelings clearly hurt. I sighed, knowing that we were not off to a good start. I don't know how else I could have said it or how I could have handled the situation any better. What could I do but either say something or have a migraine each day we worked together? I decided to press on and start teaching her the job she would be doing. I got on the computer and gave her the options she would need for our job, then gave her the handheld scanner and told her to sign on.

"How do I do that? I've never used one of these before," she said, holding the scanner away from herself.

I showed her its little keyboard. "You sign on just like you do on the computer. It is the same sign-on for any device."

She stared blankly at me. "I don't know how to sign on the computer."

"Of course you do. You would have had to use it in the accounting office. It's the same sign-on," I said, not believing what I was hearing. Could she really not understand what I was saying? She was older, probably close to retirement age, and I'm sure had not had much experience with computers. But she had been using one here since she was hired. "It's like using the computer; this is one you carry around with you. You'll have to use it back here to process claims and check in vendors." I tried to sound positive and encouraging.

She continued to stare blankly at me. "I don't know how to sign on to this. I've never used one," she insisted.

At this point, I took a deep breath and inhaled a lungful of perfume. I then tried to take deep, calming breaths without actually breathing.

My head began to pound, either from the lack of clean oxygen or from an aneurysm. My dad used to say, "You can keep quiet and let folks wonder if you are stupid or open your mouth and leave no doubt." Clearly, she was leaving me with no doubt.

I tried to show her how to sign on the scanner, showing her the keyboard and how to change from letters to numbers and put in her user ID and password. After ten minutes of complete failure, I finally just took it from her and had her tell me her user ID. This took three more tries, as she was now totally flustered and didn't seem to know how to spell her own name. She finally got it right, and I entered it in and asked for her password and got her signed in. I don't claim to be psychic, but I knew that no matter how long she would be working with me, she would never really learn one damn thing.

Every day she came in, I smelled her before I saw her. My comments about her perfume had not made any difference. She seemed to have no short-term memory at all; things I showed her were gone ten minutes later, and I had to explain them all over again. It took three weeks before she was able to sign on the handheld by herself. Lani and I had her sign-on memorized by then from helping her every day. It was exhausting working with her; we showed her how to do the same things over and over, but she never could retain it. Lani was convinced that she had some kind of memory problem. I wondered if she had some issue that kept her from concentrating. Any process that had more than three steps was a disaster.

Most spilled chemicals had to be handled a certain way that required multiple steps. I showed her how to do one bottle, very carefully going through the whole thing. I went to lunch, and when I came back, I found that she had processed out another bottle completely wrong. When I asked her about it, she said that she hadn't known what to do. I reminded her that I had shown her the whole thing only an hour before, but she had no recollection of it. I sent her to lunch and called my supervisor and told him this was not going to work; I couldn't have someone who could not learn back in my area. He said he couldn't move her already but was getting me another person for the team. I didn't care who it was, if they could just pay a little attention and learn something! He said this new girl was young but going to college, so he thought she was pretty smart. It turned out he was half-right.

Sissy was twenty, very thin and pretty, and she knew it. Lani and I called her the Pretty Princess immediately; she didn't seem to mind, and the name stuck. Soon the whole store called her that. At least she did seem to learn something; certainly she picked up on things faster than Lil, though that wasn't saying a lot. At least she wasn't afraid of the handheld; she was comfortable with it after the first day. But where that was a plus, all the life drama of an immature young adult was a big negative.

She was constantly on her phone; any text meant she had to stop what she was doing and send a reply. The phone beeped, dinged, and buzzed constantly, so productivity was slowed to a crawl. The boyfriend, ex-boyfriend, mom, dad, sister, and countless friends texted and called nonstop. I spent more time telling her to get off her phone than actually showing her how to do her job. I tried to impress upon her that since she was being paid, her job was more important than her personal life, but when you are twenty, *nothing* is more important than your personal life.

Lani and I took turns between covering the door and babysitting those two. Lil did less and less; she was happy to stand around and let someone else do the work. I tried to teach her the door. That lesson was short lived, as it did me no good for her to help me during a rush when I had to stand at her elbow and walk her through each step with every vendor. I sent her back to claims. It was much easier to let her do nothing, and at least there, she wasn't under my feet.

Pretty Princess did better at the door, as long as I could keep her focused on work, not on her phone. The main drawback was that any vendor or driver who came in under the age of thirty was completely distracted by her, too busy trying to get her name and number to do his job. More than once, I had to crush some young man's hopes and dreams by embarrassing him in front of her by pointing out some mistake or oversight he made. One got quite angry with me about it after she had walked off laughing at him; he growled at me about how mean and cruel that was, insisting I was being spiteful because I was jealous of her. I let him know that I couldn't care less about his bruised ego or what he thought of me; he was here to do a job and needed to get dates on his own time, not mine. When he kept making rude comments, I calmly told him that if he could not just do his job professionally, I would call his boss and ask for a replacement driver. He apparently figured out that I was not bluffing and let the whole thing drop. Most of those infatuated with her quickly found out that she was high maintenance and decided she wasn't quite that pretty after all.

As the holidays approached again, the back door became busier. More trucks delivered, and larger loads came daily. A special refrigerated semi-trailer was parked in one of our two unloading bays to store holiday hams, turkeys, and pies. It was a pain, because now we only had one bay for all the trucks that must be unloaded throughout the day. It causes quite a traffic jam, and you have to be extra quick checking in vendors to keep the trucks moving. The shipping trucks that deliver daily bring triple the number of boxes that also have to be checked in and then delivered around the store. And, as customers order items to be delivered to the store, all those boxes must be scanned in and then taken to the holding room at the front of the store.

Princess, Lani, and I were rushed to get all the freight checked in and delivered each day. Lil continued to be no help. I sent her to help in the clothing area, figuring rehanging and folding clothes wouldn't be too much of a mental stretch for her. I'd rather have her out doing something useful for the store than just wasting time in my area and getting paid for it. Of course, since she was using hours in my area, I couldn't get any other help.

I complained to the new store manager about it, but again, I was low on the priority list; I'd have to deal with the situation till the new year. He was neck-deep in disasters left by the two inept predecessors. But now there really was hope. I had worked with this particular store manager before and knew him well. I have worked with more managers than I can count over the years; he is the only one I would call a leader. There is a big difference between the two titles. Managers tell others to do the work; leaders get their hands dirty working with you. I had tons of respect for him already and complete faith that within a year, our *Titanic* would not only be bailed out but sailing again.

We had a lot in common: we were the same age and both had a farming background. He was a good old country boy, but very shrewd and smart. As a bonus, he was very personable and funny; he poked fun at himself and never tried to act like he was better than anyone. I jokingly called him Billy Bob Bubba in front of a group of employees one day, and he laughed and proclaimed the name suited him. Soon the whole place called him that. Bubba was a godsend; he made a few more needed changes to the management team, and soon things started to be turned around and run right. It felt good to know that we were finally headed in the right direction.

Lani, Princess, and I made it through the holidays as smoothly as we could. We were crazy busy; Lani and I divided our time between running to get things done and keeping the Princess on track and off her phone. She could learn but had no focus. When I commented on her having the attention span of a fly, she claimed it was not her fault. She loved that line and used it constantly. Nothing was ever her fault, and an excuse could always be found to back that up. Her many mistakes kept piling up; I told her if she paid half as much attention to her work as she did that phone, there would be nothing to complain about. But the phone never left her side; she'd sooner give up breathing than put it down. But for her faults, at least she was pleasant and usually cheerful, and she was not a psychopath. So, Lani and I settled in with her.

After the New Year, I once again tried to get Lil moved off my team. Bubba pulled her in the office and spoke with her about it; at first, she was happy to change areas, until she found out it would be less money to work on the sales floor. We were an area of high responsibility, so the pay was higher. Stocking shelves and rehanging clothes do not require that much thinking. She didn't want to lose pay, so she said that it was unfair to move her, claiming she had never been properly trained. When he told me, I insisted I had tried to train her, but some people were incapable of learning. He told me that to be fair to her, I would have to train her again and document each area as she learned it and then also document mistakes made. I had no choice but to do what he asked, if I wanted her moved and taken off my payroll. So, after being away from the claims area just two months, she came back, and we started back at the beginning.

I gave her the handheld scanner and asked her if she remembered the screen she needed to use. She looked blankly at it, then at me, then back at it again, the back at me. I gave her a scowl, daring her to pretend that she had never used one before. She saw my look and decided not to go that route; instead, she asked me to remind her how to sign on and what screen to use. I did, and she got signed on without a problem and opened the screen. That was as far as she was going to remember; everything else was a blank page. Everything Lani and I had shown her was completely unknown to her; when we told her that she had been shown before, she insisted that was not so. I'm sure she had convinced herself that was true; perhaps she had wiped it all out of her memory. We had to show her every process, step by step, just like before.

This time I didn't even try to show her the door; the most I did was give her keys occasionally and tell her if the bell rang to let the driver in and tell them to wait for one of us. But even that was too much; I'd go to lunch, and when I came back, I would ask if anyone was waiting to be checked in. She always had the same answer: she had no idea; how would she know if someone needed to be waited on?

"Did the bell ring? Did anyone come to the back door?" I'd ask.

"Oh, I don't know" she'd reply. "I don't think I heard a bell. Was I supposed to hear one?" We'd go through this anytime she was left alone and supposed to be listening for the bell at the back door. More than once, I found a driver or vendor waiting impatiently, and when I let them in, they would angrily tell me they had been standing outside for an hour. I'd sigh and apologize and say I had been at lunch and then get them checked in quickly. Needless to say, I only left her keys so if management asked why the door was ringing and no one was getting it, I could say I left her to cover it. Then she could not give the excuse that she had no keys to the door. She had them; she just had no idea what to do with them. Pretty much the story of her employment; she had tools and resources available but had no idea what to do with any of them.

Like Suzie, Lil's only positive was that she showed up on time, every day. Princess, on the other hand, started coming late or missing work. It's always something; you can never have a coworker who has the trifecta: cheerfulness, intelligence, and work ethic. Some people have none, some have one, and if you are lucky, some have two. But finding an employee (especially in retail) with all three is like finding a unicorn. Lil was cheerful and punctual, Princess was cheerful and had some intelligence, Lani had lots of intelligence and a great work ethic, but not so much on cheerful attitude. Attitude, yes; cheerful, no. But I liked her, being attitudinal myself. Besides, I could work with bad attitudes, as long as they worked.

I tried to keep an eye on the Lil, mostly so I could find her mistakes, document them, and then fix them. Of course, I had to fix mistakes from Princess too. Apparently, she felt if she took no responsibility for a mistake, then she didn't need to fix it either. So, I also began documenting hers, figuring I'd see who lasted longer. We soon found out why Princess was coming in late more and more often. A couple of months into the new year, she announced that she was pregnant. Lani and I did the math and realized that Princess would be out by Thanksgiving and would miss Christmas too. I spoke to Bubba and told him I needed Lil gone and a replacement in to be trained well before Princess would be gone. He assured me he was working on it, along with numerous other problems. I was on the list of things to be fixed, just closer to the bottom than the top.

18

A huge problem not yet addressed in the store was the overstock of clothing. For some reason, when we opened, about half the areas of the store started getting twice as much freight as needed. Something was entered into a computer wrong somewhere at home office, and those areas were calculated at double their size. All the other areas had been corrected; the only one left was clothing. We had been open a full year now, and about half the freight stored in the back room was clothing. We had enough to outfit the whole tristate area, and something drastic had to be done.

The best solution we had was to send our overstock to other stores; any store within 250 miles would be receiving some wonderful gifts from us. Bubba gave us a conservative estimate of seventy-five pallets that needed to be sent out. The process of sending merchandise to other stores is not something that is done much anymore. It used to be pretty standard procedure, and many managers and area leads knew the process and had helped at one time or another. It was something I had learned many years before and a process that the claims department was often involved in. But now it's rarely done. Normally stores only send things back and forth in cases of specific customer orders or special displays. What used to happen monthly now only happens a few times a year. Few know how to do it properly. And done improperly, it creates quite a mess.

Sending items from one store to another is not a complicated task, but it has a number of steps and requires some concentration to do it correctly. Therefore, Lil and Princess were going to be no help at all in getting it done. And since I was the only expert the store had on the process, some outside help would be needed to get it all done. Bubba reached out, and the state office sent June, AKA the Queen Mother. She was an expert in all policies and procedures, with over thirty years of experience. She was the keeper of solutions for any and all problems and outmatched the Diana the Dragon Lady in severity. They were good friends. Queen Mother only allowed Diana to cover for her vacations; she trusted no one else to come close to her standards.

Of course, with all my years in, I knew her well. She never had much respect for me until I became her only contact at this store who knew anything. For the entire first year, if she needed anything from our store, she called me, bypassing management completely. None of them understood what she wanted and would ask me to take care of it anyway, so she just cut out the middleman and called me first. At first when our phones were a mess and she could not get through, she asked for my cell number. She'd try the store phone first, but when someone answered and insisted that no one by my name worked there, she'd just hang up and call my cell instead. I kept it in my pocket for her and to contact vendors and shipping companies too. Since I answered her calls and did what she asked quickly and correctly, I rose in her esteem, and she now was pleasant and cheerful to me, to the amazement of everyone who knew her. She was not known for pleasant cheerfulness. But she was very good at coordinating many stores to work together when needed. She arranged to have employees from area stores come for a week of scanning, packing, and shipping out our excess clothing.

On Queen Mother's orders, I came in early on Monday to get things set up. She could be quite a control freak. Even though I knew the process, she went through it step by step, outlining exactly what she wanted. I got the full pallets of clothing staged with empty pallets beside that we could stack completed boxes on. I rounded up plenty of scanners, packing tape, and markers for the boxes and made sure my printer had plenty of paper. Lil had the day off, Princess was to keep working at claims, and Lani covered the door. Everything was as ready as I could make it.

A little after 7 a.m., some of the visiting employees started coming in. I met up with them in the back room and showed them the break room and where they could put any personal items. I saw some familiar faces that I had worked with before, and we caught up while we waited for Queen Mother, who was coming to direct the whole process. One woman I did not know started to complain loudly. She thought our store was a disgusting mess; the drive here had been too long. Why was everyone standing around waiting? If our store had any competent people, this wouldn't even be necessary. Basically, she didn't want to be there, and it only took two minutes till I didn't want her there either. I knew that they all had their own work to do, but every store needs help sometimes, and it's not that bad to go for a few days to help them out. She kept complaining, getting louder and louder, until everyone else stopped talking. When Queen Mother arrived, she silenced her with one look. She told everyone to pair up, grab a scanner and a box, and start working.

Right away, some said they didn't know how to do this process. Some stores always send someone unhelpful; they just send them anywhere so they aren't underfoot all day. Those who did know what to do helped the others, and Queen Mother pulled me aside to tell me the plan. Because our store had done so badly on our first yearly inventory last fall, all the clothing being sent out was going to be double-checked by the state compliance officer. She told me that he was bringing his own team of store security officers, and they would check every box that was done for accuracy. I wasn't too pleased, as I knew this would slow us down, but I didn't bother to argue, since there was nothing I could do about it.

Queen Mother and I came out of the claims cage to help the others scan, and she could hear that the complaining woman was at it again. She had stopped working to fuss about something and was now distracting others and bringing work to a halt. Queen Mother wasn't having it; she pulled her aside, and a few minutes later that woman grabbed her things and left to go back to her own store. I was glad. I felt there were going to be enough problems for the day without that woman being a pain. Unfortunately, the problems started immediately.

The whole process should not have been that hard. In the correct screen on the scanner, you first put in the sending store number, then the receiving store number. At this point, the system assigns your box an invoice number, which you write on the outside of the box. Then you scan each item you are sending, double-check your piece count for accuracy, then finalize. Each box should be done separately; it makes it much easier to find any mistakes. It's a whole lot easier to check twenty pieces instead of one hundred. After you finalize, two copies of the invoice print, one for the sending store records and one to go in the box with the items for the receiving store.

Queen Mother assigned each duo a receiving store number; they were to take a whole pallet, and every box on that pallet would go to the same store. When they finished with one pallet, it would be checked by the security team, then all boxes taped up, the pallet wrapped for shipping, and moved out of the way. Then they would go to another pallet and get a different store number from her. That was the plan, which should not have been that hard to follow. But in retail, very little goes according to plan.

Every mistake is fixable; you just have to know how to fix it or know who knows how to fix it. With all my years, there is very little I don't know how to fix. I'm not afraid of making mistakes; sometimes it is one of the best ways to learn. And I know how to fix almost anything because I've seen almost everything. (You never say you have seen it all—someone will take that as a challenge.)

The main thing with sending items is that once you input everything and finalize it, it is a done deal. There is no way to adjust or change it;

you have to reverse everything you just did and redo the whole thing correctly. Most stores only have a few employees who really know how to do it properly. I have done thousands of item sending/receivings over the years and have become quite an expert on how to fix it when they are done wrong. Queen Mother was closely watching the group, trying to head off the potential problems before it became a huge mess. No such luck. It was a lovely spring week that turned into a nightmare. Just trying to send out as much merchandise as we needed to do with this many people in just a week's time was the first level of hell.

Problem one: (Second level of hell.) The first thing one duo did was forget their receiving store number. This can be quite an issue, when you finalize, the computer system tells the store number you entered that these items are on the way. This tells the receiving store to expect these items to add to their inventory. When you then send the items to a different store, obviously it causes a lot of confusion. Then the store that got the items will call and complain and receive them while the store that expected them must hand-key the list of items back to me so I can input it for the store that actually got the pallet.

Problem two: (Third level of hell.) Almost no one wrote down their invoice number on each box. The invoice that prints must be matched up with the correct box, so it can be verified and so the receiving store can check and accept the box correctly. Obviously, it's a whole lot faster to just match the invoice number than to try to visually verify each item to each paper. Especially when everyone is scanning the same things, like clothing!

Problem three: (Fourth level of hell.) The extra step of each box being verified by the security team. The team, led by the state compliance officer, had to wait till there were boxes to check before they could get to work. So, instead of just waiting thirty minutes for some boxes to be ready, they decided to stand around in our way, talking loudly about nothing, bothering and distracting some of the duos, and just generally being obnoxious. The compliance officer also decided that none of the invoices should be finalized until his team had checked them. Since he believed he and his team were much smarter than the rest of us, they could then find and fix all our mistakes before the invoices were finalized and it was too late. Queen Mother told him that he and his team had better be standing by to verify boxes quickly, so this whole process could keep moving. He, of course, didn't actually verify anything; he left that to his team. Like most state officers, he had risen above the level of physical work and into the plane of delegation. I already had doubts about how good his team was, and they set out to prove they were smarter than us by finding mistakes in every single box they checked, even the ones done by myself and the Queen Mother. I didn't bother to argue; I was sure I had not made mistakes but knew it wouldn't do any good to question them. Queen Mother, on the other hand, had no intention of letting anyone tell her she had done something wrong. So, she made them check her box again with her, and when it turned out she was correct, she then insisted they recheck what they had already checked again. It turned out a big part of their mistakes was due to mistake number two; they were not making sure the sheet matched the box before they began.

And so, within two hours of starting, the whole plan had come off the rails. I wasn't all that surprised by this; anytime you get a large group of employees working on something, it has to be led with an iron fist or chaos happens. Queen Mother would have been fine as the iron fist, but the state officer just had to butt in, and now we had a mess. She called the state officer over and demanded that he get his team in line and on track. This was very embarrassing for him, to be called out in front of a bunch of lowly employees, so to try to save face, he called for a lunch break and took his team with him. He ordered us not to finalize any boxes until they got back, just to leave everything open and ready to check. We could print a trial copy of the invoice paper that was to go in each box for them. Maybe he thought they all had low blood sugar and some food would help them get their heads in the game. I had my doubts. We all continued to work a couple more hours until Queen Mother called for lunch; when she visited, you went to lunch when she said. She and I had to continually go to the computer and delete invoices that were opened for the wrong store numbers (when it was caught) and looked to see the growing list of open invoices waiting for the security team. After a few hours of work by this large team, there were over one hundred invoices opened. She ordered everyone to finish the box they were on, and we all went to get lunch. I already had a feeling of dread in my stomach about how the morning had gone. If I had known what was coming, I would have never come back from lunch.

Problem four: (Fifth level of hell.) Open invoices are automatically deleted from the system if left open too long. (We didn't know that would happen.) When we came back, Queen Mother and I went to check the screen and planned to print any trial reports needed for boxes that didn't have sheets yet. To our horror, the screen was empty; all the invoices were gone. I didn't know if I wanted to scream or cry. In truth, I wanted to do both and then leave this mess for someone else to clean up. While we were sitting there in shock, the state officer and his team finally came back from their two-and-a-half-hour lunch break. He breezed in the claims cage, his ego restored from food, and his team laughing at his dumb jokes. "Let's get this going. I don't have all day to fix what you all have messed up," he said with a laugh. Queen Mother spun around in the chair and glared at him with such force, I expected him to burst into flame. "They are gone! All the open invoices are gone!" she said furiously. Since the normal procedure is to finalize a box as soon as you are done with it, no one knew that the system would delete any left open more than an hour. I guess it was supposed to be some kind of failsafe. If someone opened an invoice but left it because they didn't know what they were doing, the system would delete it before it became a problem to fix. This failsafe had just destroyed our entire morning of work, and there was absolutely nothing we could do but start all over.

Starting over: (Sixth level of hell.) Only about twenty boxes had been verified and finalized properly before the security team ran away for lunch. Those boxes were okay, but everything else had to rescanned and reboxed. So, we started back at the beginning while Queen Mother spoke to the state officer. Technically, he was her superior, but not on this. She ordered that he and his team would *not* be checking each box; that took too much time, and the last thing we needed was this cycle repeated. They would spot-check five boxes on each pallet and leave it at that. Duos found making too many mistakes would be monitored closely; those without mistakes would just be left to scan and finalize their boxes themselves. Of course, duos who had made mistakes one and two before lunch kept right on making them. Queen Mother was constantly trying to find and delete invoices for the wrong stores, but of course, if you can't get the store number right, you sure aren't going to have the invoice number right. So, she ended up deleting invoices that other people were working on because some idiot gave her the wrong invoice number. Now those who were doing okay were yelling that their invoice disappeared in the middle of scanning a box.

Starting over the start over: (Seventh level of hell.) At this point, everything was in chaos. Everyone was yelling, cursing, and throwing things; we had all reached our breaking point. Queen Mother tried to regain control and called us all together. We all got quiet to listen. No one really wished to add her wrath to this disastrous situation. When the Queen Mother stood at the front of the class, looking over her glasses at you, you had better for the love of God shut your pie hole. She outlined her new plan to at least get us through this day. Any store numbers that had no boxes ready were being abandoned; we'd start on those tomorrow. Those store numbers with boxes ready would be checked that each invoice was finalized and that the sheet was in the box. Those would be taped shut and ready to ship. Then we would all work together on those store numbers to make full pallets. We did as we were told and managed to get four pallets of clothes ready to ship. Her goal for the day had been twenty pallets. The group cleaned up the boxes and restacked them, getting ready for day two. Suddenly about half the group had excuses why they could not come back the next day or the rest of the week. I was hardly surprised, and frankly, I didn't blame them. She found out who was willing to come back and try again tomorrow and then sent them all home.

She came into the claims cage to talk damage control with me. There was a large pile of invoice sheets that we had to correct. Some of them still needed to be deleted from the system, some needed to be verified that there was a finalized box to go with it, and some were for the wrong store number, meaning I'd have to call that store and explain what went wrong and work with them to fix it. It was past time for Lani to go home, but she had seen the train wreck and stayed to help me. She and I quickly went through the pallets and made sure that each box had its sheet and that we had our store copy too. Queen Mother started the job of calling stores to alert them of the mess-ups; we would have to fax them a copy of the invoice sheet, and they would have to manually receive it in their system (which meant hand typing each UPC code), then resend it back to our store (hand typing it all again). Obviously, any store that got a call was not pleased at the extra work but didn't dare complain to the Queen Mother about it.

It took Lani and me about an hour to finish our task. Queen Mother had made calls on process of elimination, comparing store numbers on the invoices with her master list. That left the open ones to be deleted, which we quickly did. When there were no more open invoices, we called it a day. We'd try again tomorrow and pray things went at least a little smoother.

The next day, I came in early again, doing what I could to set us up for success. Lani once more covered the door while Princess covered claims. At 7 a.m., ten employees from other stores came in, most from yesterday and a few new. We all agreed that there would not be a repeat of the day before. Most of those who had helped cause problems one and two did not come back, either by their choice or Queen Mother's. She came in soon afterward and got us lined out again. We spread out a little more this time. I think she hoped if the duos couldn't chat with the others, they might pay more attention to their work. Also, the state officer and his team were absent; he had meetings all day, and his team didn't want to face the Queen Mother without him, so they didn't show. That was fine with all of us; they certainly hadn't helped the day before. So, the process began again; Queen Mother would assign each duo a store number, and they were to write the invoice number on each box. This time we could finalize each box as we went and then move on to another. This went pretty smoothly through the morning. When a duo would fill a pallet, they would be assigned a new store number and start again. One duo started putting in the wrong store number again; Queen Mother quickly separated them and put each one with someone more experienced. That seemed to solve the issue, and work continued on track until a new problem appeared.

Problem five: (Eighth level of hell.) To put the invoice sheet in each and every box meant that there was a constant parade in the claims cage to the printer, then a discussion and debate about which sheet belonged to which duo. Queen Mother was supposed to be organizing the sheets by store number but had gotten a call about a problem in another store and was on the phone, trying to help them. She kicked everyone out of the cage and told them to just go on, and she would give them the sheets later. They just needed to label the pallet with the store number, and all the sheets for that store could be put in a large envelope and put with the pallet when shipped. The receiving store could easily match the sheets with the invoice numbers on the boxes and it would be fine. In theory, that should have worked. In practice, what actually happened was that most of the boxes did not have the invoice number written on them, and then one duo wrote the wrong store number on their pallet. Then, when we went to lunch, someone decided to clean up and started putting all the different boxes on the floor on one big pallet. Somehow no one noticed this when we got back; I didn't because I had just finished my pallet before we left and was ready to start a new one and didn't have any boxes left on the floor. None of the duos questioned anything; they just all started over on new pallets, like everything was fine.

So, about an hour before the end of the day, Queen Mother called me and had me call for a truck to come and pick up all the pallets that were ready. Everyone had been working together quickly to make up for the lack of progress the day before, and we were all proud to see that there was a total of nineteen pallets to be shipped, four from Monday and fifteen from today. We started to try to match her huge pile of sheets with the correct pallets, and that's when we started to discover the new mess we had. Some pallets had no store number, some boxes had no invoice numbers, and at least one pallet had boxes for every store mixed together. Queen Mother and I were in a panic; we had less than an hour till the help would leave and only about two hours before the shipping truck would arrive to sort it all out. Lani came to help, and everyone started tearing pallets apart, desperate for a number to match any sheet to.

I knew my pallets were okay, but I sure didn't trust anyone else's. We did our best, but I knew that about half the pallets had sheets missing completely or sheets for the wrong boxes attached. Most of the group were nice and stayed late to try to put the pallets back together correctly, but when the shipping truck arrived and they had to be loaded or left behind, Queen Mother still had a dozen or so sheets in her hand. She called it, telling us to just wrap it all and send it, and we'd have to sort it out with the receiving stores later. Of course, when she said "we'd," she really meant me. My time in hell was nowhere close to over.

Wednesday morning, when the group showed up, there were only six. Queen Mother was done with the mistakes; she only asked the best to come and help finish. We still had a good forty pallets of clothes to send out, but with this team, we thought we could do it in two days. We all jumped in. This time there were no duos; we were all capable of working on our own. Plus, we were all sick of the stupid mistakes from the last two days. Everyone put their head down and got busy. There was no talking with this group, just scanning. Queen Mother was pleased; we were pushing through the boxes at a record pace. Finally, all seemed to be going to plan. We rocked out twenty-two pallets that day without a hitch. We got them all wrapped with their sheets and shipped out and gave ourselves a well-deserved pat on the back. We would finish up tomorrow.

The same six came back on Thursday, and we started again. By now, some of the receiving stores were getting their pallets, and the angry phone calls started coming in. Queen Mother took those, calmly explaining what each store would have to do to correct the mistakes. They grumbled but didn't dare argue with her. She also was calling around to see what other stores might take some of these clothes off our hands. She had finally reached the end of her list of store numbers. No one else wanted the clothes, so we were told to start using some of the same store numbers over again. She told us that stores eleven, twelve, and twenty-one would take more pallets, so we should start scanning more boxes for them.

Problem six: (Ninth level of hell.) By now, you can probably guess what happened. When we went to match up the invoice sheets with the pallets, we soon discovered disaster had struck again. Someone transposed their store number, someone else forgot to write their invoice numbers on boxes, and another got confused and kept switching back and forth between stores twelve and twenty-one. Once again we were scrambling, trying to get it all matched before the shipping truck arrived. And once again we ended up just slapping any leftover sheets onto any leftover pallet and sending it out. All the rest cared about was that they were done coming to my store. They had done their damage and could go home, while I had to pick up the pieces. Since Queen Mother was standing beside me, I kindly thanked them all for their help as they left. I didn't feel like thanking anyone, I knew it would take me weeks to get everything straightened out.

Queen Mother and I went through the paperwork, separating piles of what should be okay with what we knew was not. I put it all in a large box, labeled it "clothing pallet hell," and clocked out for the day. I had had enough; I wasn't dealing with any more problems right now.

Problem seven: (Tenth level of hell.) I spent the next week on the computer and the phone, taking calls from angry stores, walking them through the fixes, and making corrections on my end. The screw-up pile got smaller; of course, some stores didn't fix the fix correctly and caused me to do yet another fix on my end. Since all the clothes had been shipped out, any corrections had to be hand-keyed on the scanner. My ten-key skills were brought back out and served me well. Every store that called me was furious about the stupid mistakes and how they would have to spend their time fixing them; furious with me until I told them about my week and how dark and depressing the final level of hell is. Furious until I told them that in four days, we had sent out almost eighty pallets of clothes to forty-three stores, and almost every pallet had mistakes that I would have to fix. Then they were very sympathetic and understood the mountain of work I still had to do. Only one store still cursed me; the woman on the line called me an inept, stupid moron and insisted she would file a complaint with home office against me. I told her to knock herself out; that sounded like the least of my problems right now. She insisted on my supervisor's name, saying she would call them too and tell them what an idiot I was. I smiled to myself and gave her the number to Queen Mother and wished her good luck as she hung up on me. How I would have loved to listen in on that conversation!

Queen Mother had been calling me every day for a progress report on how the corrections were coming. I knew she would keep hounding me till every mistake had been fixed. When she called later that day, the first thing she asked was if I had told the cranky woman to call her. I admitted I had; I told her that cranky had cussed me and called me stupid and wanted to know who put me in charge of this mess. I thought the best one to speak to her was the Queen Mother; no one knew more about what we had gone through than her. I asked how the phone call went and laughed as she told me how cranky had started in cussing and fussing at her and how Queen Mother had shut her down. When she found out that Queen Mother was not just some green manager with no experience but a highly respected, knowledgeable, and very valuable member of our state team, cranky had to change her attitude and decided that she should just make the necessary corrections and be done with it. She may have been rude, but she was smart enough to realize she was not going to win a fight with the Queen Mother.

By the end of the week, I had finished making my needed calls to stores about the mess, but I was still getting calls from stores about how to fix items they had received and needed to scan in. If I hadn't already been an expert, I surely would have been one by now. I took the opportunity to teach Lani and Princess about the process. Lani was familiar but had not done very many; Princess was brand new to it. I carefully went through the whole thing step by step, especially highlighting what not to do. I also wrote out detailed instructions on how to send out items and how to scan them in from other stores for future reference and included how to troubleshoot problems and make corrections. I put the sheets in the big book and made copies that I faxed and emailed to many other stores for their use. Queen Mother had me send it to every store in the area, hoping to never see a repeat. By the end of the month, I had quit getting phone calls and declared my time in hell to be over.

19

Shortly after I emerged from hell, another blessing happened. Lil was finally moved off my team permanently. I had gathered enough evidence of her mistakes that Bubba called her in and explained that she could either change areas or stay and lose her job from her mistakes. She wisely chose to move and joined the clothing area, where she had been helping anyway. That was the good news. The bad news was that I was not going to get a replacement; home office was doing a big shakeup of how and when payroll hours should be used, and since Lani, Princess, and I were doing fine with just the three of us, hours for my area had been cut. I reminded Bubba that Princess would be gone right around the holidays for her maternity leave, and he said he would try to get us some help when the time came. I knew what that really meant was he would expect Lani and me to just handle it all ourselves. The chances of getting some help were slim to none.

There were two main reasons for this; every area of the store was going to want help for the holiday time, and claims/receiving isn't a place you can just throw someone. Everything we do is specialized to our areas and requires training. Unlike the sales floor, where each area runs on the same guidelines, claims and shipping/receiving are specialty areas that no one knows how to do unless they actually work there. So, even if Bubba did throw someone back to help us, they really would be no help at all, since they wouldn't have the first clue what to do, and we would have no time to show them. I told Lani all this, and knew she wouldn't be happy about it, but at least we could rely on each other. And sometimes that is just enough to get you through a rough season.

The summer went on, and even though she didn't look pregnant, Princess suffered from every known pregnancy symptom there was. The morning sickness meant she had a great excuse to be late every day; food cravings meant she had to take many breaks for snacks; ankles swelling and feeling tired meant she had to sit very often; and lack of concentration and focus meant she had "pregnancy brain." She played these to the hilt; it was a golden opportunity for her to do as little as possible and get paid for it.

I used this time to practice a system that would let Lani and I keep up on all the work together. I took over at the door. I was a little faster, and more problems tend to happen there that I would normally be called to handle anyway. Plus, I had more patience with drivers and vendors than Lani did. I would be more forgiving of inexperience or technical problems than she. She would cover claims first, and then help me when the door got busy. Then I'd go to lunch, and then she would, and then we'd both finish up claims in the afternoon before we went home. We juggled it all pretty well. The main problem was that Princess was our weekend person, and when she was out, one of us would have to at least work Saturday, which would leave the other one alone one day of the week. Weekdays are much busier for us than the weekend, but at least five companies do a Saturday delivery, so someone has to cover the door. Bubba decided that no one would work on Sunday; claims is supposed to be manned seven days a week, but that would just have to slide. Lani and I discussed it and decided that Thursdays were the quietest day, so that would be a day one of us would work alone. We would take turns working Saturdays, so one week we would work a long week and the next a short week. This process started a little earlier than we intended, as now Princess liked to call in on the weekends. Since we were both there during the week, she didn't have to do much. But since she was scheduled alone on the weekends, any work happening had to be done by her. When management started to make comments about how nothing seemed to be getting done (everyone had been hearing her pregnancy excuses for eight months and were sick of them), she started to just call in sick instead. So, Lani or I would get a call early most Saturday mornings, asking if one of us could come in and take care of the vendors. There were only two managers who even tried to muddle through the process; the rest just called us or sent the vendor away to come back during the week. Though she wasn't actually due till Christmastime, Princess was ready to be off work and got a doctor's note that she needed to be on bedrest. So, the week of Thanksgiving, she took leave, and Lani and I were officially on our own.

The days just got busier and busier. Everything was hectic; everyone in the store was overworked and irritable. When you are short-handed, management promises to ease up your workload and not drop extra duties on you. This is a lie. They avoid you for a couple of days, and you think maybe they will leave you alone. But the workload never stops growing, and pretty soon, more gets piled on your plate. Then you come in one morning, and two pallets of home appliances need to be sent to another store. Of course, nothing is said to your face about it; they know you will be angry and yell, and they don't want to hear it, so it is left after you go home, with a scrawled note for you to take care of it. Actually, you are lucky if there is a note; most managers like to leave no evidence behind, just the pile of work they want done. A note might be traced back to them, leading you to the culprit. I believe that crime shows have played a part in the breakdown of communication in the workplace. If a person leaves no evidence, then they can't be charged with any wrongdoing, and they can deny any knowledge of how this work got dumped on Lani and me. So, most times things are just left in and around the claims cage, and we are supposed to figure out who left it, why it was left, and what needs to be done with it. I have spent far too much time doing detective work to discover the truth when five seconds to write a damn note would save my time and aggravation.

The note on the home appliances pallets just said, "send out." Lani and I were immediately pissed, and I told her to ignore the pallets and get to work. We were not going to touch them till somebody said something about them. Then the fireworks would start.

It was almost the end of our day before one of the managers stopped by. He was not one of my favorites; he had become a manager to avoid physical labor. He had also been raised with no manners. *Please* and *thank you* were words he was not familiar with. He stopped, and in his usual blunt manner, asked me what I was going to do about the "stuff." I knew what he meant but pretended I didn't.

"What stuff? There is a lot of stuff in this back room. Maybe you could be more specific."

He answered in his usual rude way. "Those pallets over there that need to be sent out. Didn't you see them?"

I decided I would match his rudeness. "I saw them. And I saw the note that says *send out*. Do you have a destination in mind, or should I pick one at random? Maybe I should just pull a store number out of my ass."

He ignored my reply. "There is a note on the pallets. Did you bother to read it? It will tell you where to send them."

"I did read it. Obviously, you have not. Like I said, the note says *send out*. That is all." I went and got the note and handed it to him. "Do you see anything on the note indicating where these should be sent? Am I missing some hidden message? Is there a secret code hidden in those two words?" I said as condescendingly as possible.

"You don't have to be rude about it. You could have called one of us and asked."

"I don't have time to waste on stupid crap. Whoever wrote this note could have taken one more second and written a store number on it. Then I would have just taken care of the pallets, and we would not be having this conversation at all. But, fine. I'm asking you. Where should these pallets be sent?"

He spoke into his radio. "Does anyone know where these pallets by claims are supposed to be sent to? There is no store number on the note."

We waited a few seconds, and Bubba came back to the claims cage. He told me the store number and asked to see the note. I handed it to him, and he just shook his head. I told him that the pallets would go out tomorrow; it was too late in the day to get them scanned out and shipped. I also told him that I would have taken care of it today if there had been a store number on the note, but since we were short-handed, I didn't have time to play Sherlock Holmes and try to figure it out. I let him know that Lani and I would not be touching anything that did not have a clear note on it with how the items should be handled. He agreed that was fair, and he took the note, saying he would address the problem. This is why I liked him so much: he didn't pass the blame; he just tried to correct the problem so he wouldn't have to deal with it again. Of course, we did still get things back without notes, but not as many. Some people just refuse to take any chance they might have to take responsibility for their actions.

This kind of thing went on regularly, but somehow Lani and I made it through to the new year. We supported each other daily, propping each other up and keeping a steady supply of chocolate on hand.

20

Halfway through January, Princess finally came back to work from her maternity leave. She was excited to be a new mom but was exhausted trying to juggle an infant, college, and working part time. While she had never taken her job seriously, before the baby, we were at the bottom of her priority list. Now we weren't on the list at all. She couldn't afford a daycare, so her new son was left with family members. Unfortunately, most were no more reliable than she was. When no one would agree to watch them, she called in. So, Lani and I were not much better off than when Princess was gone. The main difference was that Princess was to be working the weekends again, so we didn't have to. But with her poor attendance, we still got called at least once a month to cover Saturday. I complained to Bubba about it, but he thought Princess had potential and wanted me to mentor her. I sure didn't see it but promised I would try.

She had only been back a few months when she announced that one of her classes was taking a trip to Europe. They would be gone for three weeks in June. She told us and then asked if we would like to contribute to her trip and fund her dreams of going to Europe. I literally laughed out loud. Lani was shocked that she would have the nerve to ask us. I wasn't surprised at that; it's just the mindset of someone who feels they are entitled to whatever they want. We just told her that we would not be contributing. She was quite put out, telling us how mean we were not to help her reach for her dreams. Lani informed her that she quit having selfish dreams when she started having children; now her dreams should be for giving her kids a better life. Princess stomped off, tossing her long hair. Bubba passed her in the hallway and took a detour to claims, to find out what was going on. He had seen that she was upset and asked what happened. When we told him, he could not believe his ears that she had really asked us for money. Plus, he was disgusted that she planned to be gone for three weeks; she only showed up for about half her shifts now. He just shook his head and told us that if she came to him crying that we were mean, he would ignore it. Of course, we barely saw her the rest of the day. She spent her time telling her sob story to anyone who would listen. The next day, she had brushed it off and was back to her normal self.

When I say *normal*, that is, of course, a relative term. What was normal for the Princess was to be living with her head floating two feet above the rest of her body. Some days she was quite entertaining. Besides her phone, her favorite plaything was her hair. She had long, straight hair and was constantly messing with it. If it was down, she would put it up, but then she decided she didn't like it and would take it back down. Then she might braid it or just leave it in a ponytail, but never just leave it alone. One day she complained of a headache. I asked her if she wanted something for it. My chronic foot pain causes me to keep over-the-counter pain relievers on hand. She took some and declared the reason for her headache was that her hair was too heavy, piled up in a bun on top of her head. I can often get a headache at work, but mine is usually from some coworker, never because my hair is too heavy. I offered to solve the problem with a pair of scissors. I could lighten her load in a minute. She refused and spent another ten minutes rearranging her hair. Anytime she complained about it, I reached for the scissors, and she quickly moved away.

I did my best to mentor her as Bubba wished. She could learn and understand the processes that needed to be done; she was not a stupid girl. But she just refused to apply herself to doing her job well. I was teaching her how to send a damaged item back to the supplier; some companies want their products sent back to be repaired. We were going through the whole process (which was taking forever, since she could not pay attention to me instead of her phone) of scanning the item out, making a claim invoice, finalizing that invoice and packaging the item for shipping. She had to get on the computer to create and print a shipping label for the box. I was showing her how to input the address and then measure the box to put in the dimensions. She also needed to put in the weight of the box; the program then calculates the cost to ship the box. She asked me how much to put in for the weight, and I told her to take a guess, since she was the one packaging it.

She stared blankly at me. "How on earth should I know how much this weighs? We should have a scale in here for that."

"It's not that hard to guess. A sixteen-ounce can of corn weighs about one pound. Decide if the box weighs more or less than that." By now I just wanted to finish the lesson.

Now she stared at the box. "How am I supposed to guess?"

"You could try picking it up. That is often the first step in trying to determine how much something weighs."

She sat there, looking at me in disbelief. "I still don't know how you expect me to guess."

At this point, I ran out of patience. "For the love of God, just pick up the stupid box and guess!"

She shook her head at me and finally picked up the box. "I have no idea how much this weighs. It's impossible for me to know that!" she said, shaking the box at me.

"Just give it here." I took it and balanced it in my hand. "Put in three pounds. That will be close enough. I told you, it's a guess." Lani walked in at this moment in the cage and stopped to watch.

She tossed her hair dramatically. "I really don't know how you expect me to guess these things. My hand is not a scale!"

She stomped out of the room as Lani and I just looked at each other and cracked up laughing. We were still laughing about it when she came back. By then, her tantrum had blown over. It became an office joke. Every time Princess would ask me some silly question, I would ask her, "How should I know that? My hand is not a scale!" and Lani and I would laugh some more. Princess didn't seem upset about our teasing. Lani thought she just didn't care, but I wondered if she just didn't understand that we were making fun of her. She was a pretty easy target; she said something dingy weekly.

One day, Bubba was looking over some reports in the claims cage when Princess came in and set her scanner down. She pulled her hairbrush out of her purse and redid her hair again. She finished with her hair and went back out to continue working. Suddenly, she yelled at me, mad that I had hidden her scanner. I was working at the computer the whole time and told her so. She stormed in, mad that I was playing a joke on her and demanding that I give her scanner back. I repeated that I didn't have it and asked where she left it. She turned around and saw it on the table where Bubba was working, right where she had set it down. She went to pick it up, and Bubba told her "It's okay, Princess. You are so pretty" in the most patronizing tone. Again, I cracked up, and Bubba chuckled as she gave him a look and left the room.

Bubba was pretty funny; he liked a good joke and didn't take himself too seriously either. He and I joked a lot since we had known each other for about five years now. Lani was helping me at the door one day when he came by. I called him over, telling him that an envelope had arrived for him. He thanked me as he took it and jokingly said he hoped it was the latest copy of some porn magazine. It wasn't. Lani and I cracked up as he opened it to see it was a handbook from home office about sexual harassment in the workplace. We howled with laughter as his face got red, and he noted that his timing could not have been better. We agreed.

When Princess came back from her trip to Europe, she started planning for her next semester of college. She felt very inspired by her trip and now declared that she wanted to be a teacher. Lani and I were pretty sure that would never happen, but it was her choice. I asked her if she was working with her older son; he was three and about to start preschool. It would be good training for her to work with him. She said that he knew most of his colors, and she was trying to teach him shapes and numbers up to ten. Princess showed us how she drew a straight line on a paper and told him that it meant one. She skipped two (she hadn't figured out how to explain it yet) and then drew three lines that connected at the corners. This was three, she explained, and three makes a triangle. Lani and I just stared at her. She showed us again and said that three makes a triangle. We just shook our heads, not quite sure what we had just heard. I suggested that she stop trying to teach him things and leave it for preschool. It became another one of her lines we used. Anytime something happened that was too stupid to be explained, Lani and I would look at each other and remark how "three makes a triangle."

As time went on, her attendance got worse and worse. She constantly wanted her schedule changed but then would not come in for her shifts. She also complained to Bubba that he needed to make her full time so she could get more hours and benefits. I told him that she didn't come in for half her shifts now; how on earth did he think she would show up for more? Plus, she changed when she was available to work. She didn't want to work on Sunday anymore, so it could be family day. She kept crying about it till Bubba lost his cool, telling her that to be full time, you had to work at least X number of hours a week, and she wasn't even available to work that many. He and I discussed moving her out of my area and replacing her. It was fall, and I told him it would be really nice to have some reliable help during the holidays, for once. He agreed, and the next week, when she complained to him about wanting full time (and yet needing more days off), he took the chance to tell her that since she could no longer work the schedule required for the claims area, she would be moved to the sales floor. She tried to fight it; the only reason she wanted to stay put was claims was a higher pay rate. He told her she was free to try, but she was moving, whether she liked it or not. She got moved to the clothing area, as they always needed help. She hated it and continued to call in and miss work. By the time the holidays were over, she had lost her job for poor attendance. Lani and I were not surprised.

21

Her replacement started with Lani and me in December. It's a lousy time to try to train someone new, but Cathy was pretty good at learning and kept a positive attitude. We had requested her, and it proved that Christmas is the season of miracles that we actually got her. Normally, if you request a certain person for your area, the immediate reaction from management is *no*. Obviously, you are only requesting that person because you are friends, not because you happen to know that they are smart, hardworking, and show up.

We called her Jingles. She got her nickname because each year for the holidays, she tries to cover herself in jingle bells. She puts them on her shoes, on hair bows, bracelets, necklaces, pretty much wherever she can think. She does it because she enjoys showing her Christmas spirit, and it also annoys the crap out of all the Scrooges in the store.

Of course, when you work in retail, it is really hard to enjoy the holidays. The workload increases, as there are even more products to stock, plus lots of specialty things only sold at Christmastime. More customers flood the store, and all of them are in a hurry to get what they want and get out. Most employees are asked to work overtime. It adds to your paycheck but takes away time you could spend with your family. Plus, most large retailers extend their hours, staying open later or extra days. Christmas Day was the only day I was guaranteed off each year.

You could hear Jingles coming five aisles away. On the other hand, Lani is part ninja, part cat. I made her wear a set of door keys just so she couldn't sneak up on me. I have excellent hearing, but without those keys, she could appear behind me without a sound. Jingles was a very cheerful but sensitive woman. When she left the sales floor, some of the other area supervisors were mad and would make mean comments to her. Plus, no matter how nice she was, right away they started saying how she was just as mean as Lani and me. This really bothered her. I just reminded her that you will never suit everyone, so there is no use in trying. Lani and I tried to teach her to just ignore all the talk and stay away from the store gossips.

Jingles is like me, in that we really beat ourselves up if we do something wrong. You are expected to make mistakes your first month, but she would get very upset and feel terrible if I had to fix some mistake she made. I told her that mistakes happen to us all, and as time goes on, she would make fewer and then fix those she did make.

Shortly after Jingles joined us, we lost Bubba. He was transferred to another store that was in trouble; he had done so well turning our store around, he was now expected to do it again. It sucked. When he told Lani and me that he was being moved, we hugged him and told him how much we would miss him. We even teared up, something I have never done over any other manager. He told us that he would be back to visit, and we could always stop in the other store and see him. He tried to soften the blow by telling us that his replacement was a lot like him, and we would barely notice the difference. It took only days to notice a huge difference, and I could foresee us losing most of the ground our store had finally made up.

Our new manager, Dirk, was about fifteen years younger than Bubba, loud and cocky, and never let go of his cell phone. He would walk around staring at it, look up for a moment as he passed an employee and give you a very loud "Good morning!" and then look right back at the phone and keep walking. He gave the appearance of being friendly and cheerful without actually interacting with anyone. I've seen the same behavior before, and I knew the whole act really means that he wants to be able to say that he is friendly and speaks to his people while not really speaking to anyone at all. He certainly had no intention of stopping to listen to any problem or concern you might have. He quickly made it clear that he expected everyone to use the chain of command; you were to go to your immediate supervisor with any problem and leave him out of it.

Dirk was quick to take credit for any positive thing happening; any problem was definitely not his fault. And since he would not listen to or solve any problems, he gave us the impression that he just didn't care. And when the store manager does not care (or at least looks like it to his employees), you really can't expect hourly people to care either. And no matter how dedicated an employee is, they cannot care enough to hold up the whole store. It also drags morale down; Bubba had worked hard to raise morale and expect his employees to take pride in their store. Thanks to Dirk, it was now dropping like a stone.

Dirk was a true manager. He hid in his office, barked orders over the radio, delegated absolutely everything, and never missed a lunch or taking his days off. Like so many managers I had seen before him, he seemed to have the opinion that he had risen to the lofty heights and now should be able to just sit back and look down on his peons and watch them do all the work. It was bad enough that he had to step down and walk among us for a few minutes each day; he had no intention of sticking around to help get anything done.

I am always amazed at that attitude, as if we are still in the Middle Ages, with lords and peasants. I wish more managers would study history; maybe they would learn that eventually the peasants got sick of being told to do more work for less wages, and a revolt would happen. They might attack, behead the lord, and burn the castle to the ground. Today's equivalent is that employees stop coming to work, start doing less work, and spread a negative attitude everywhere they go. The end result is the same: the kingdom (or store) fails. When that happens now, instead of being beheaded, the manager will lose his store and get transferred to another (as happened with Gary and Donny). Then they get to start over, blaming their previous failure on the bad employees who caused all the problems; it certainly couldn't have been their fault. The problem is that by just moving them, they don't learn anything about why they failed. If they were demoted (or fired), they would have to work their way back up and just might learn a lesson or two about how to lead their employees to success. But a demotion rarely happens. Most times, the manager is just moved, his butt-kissing skills saving his job.

It also became clear that Dirk played favorites. You could be a favorite if you were either a thin, not-too-bright twenty-something female or a yes man. Like most men in any power position, he believed that anyone who laughed at his jokes and agreed with everything he said must be almost as smart as himself. Actually, it shows they are smarter; they know just what to do to get a raise and a promotion without doing any work to earn it. And of course, what powerful man doesn't want thin, pretty girls fawning over him?

Since I didn't fit either of those groups, you might think I would be worried for my job. But I wasn't; I had spent my years learning as much as I could to make myself valuable. No matter his personal feelings about me, he needed me. No one in that store knows as much as I do about the old computer system. I've been hearing for about five years now that the old system will no longer be used, as everything on it will be obsolete. It still hasn't happened; more programs get removed each year, but there are still a number of things that are done on the old system only. Until new programs are written to take on those tasks, the old system will have to be used. And since I'm the store expert on it, Dirk won't make any move to get rid of me, much as he might like to.

Like most managers, he really has no idea of the ins and outs of the computer system, especially the old system. So, it's not unusual for a manager to come up and tell you to do things that are not possible and then argue when you tell them you can't do it.

Dirk came back to the claims cage one day. "Hey there! I need you to do something. I need you to put this new beer product on file, so we can sell it here."

"I can't do that," I said matter-of-factly.

He ignored my answer. "Have you tried this? It's great. It's in the liquor stores, but I want us to sell it here too. If you try it, I know you'll love it!"

"I can't do that," I said again.

Apparently, he thought I was pulling his leg. Surely, I would not refuse to do as he asked. "What? Of course, you can. Here is the UPC code. That's all you need, right?"

Now I was irritated. "First of all, no, that is not all I would need to put an item on file. Second, I cannot put beer items on file; we are not allowed to do that."

"What are you talking about? Are you saying you don't know how to do it?" His voice grew louder as he got impatient.

I raised my voice, trying to make him listen. "Of course I know how to do it. Listen to me. No one can put beer items on file; the system will not allow it. It's not allowed by home office because of ATF rules. Do you hear me? I cannot put that item on file."

He glared at me, refusing to believe that something he wants done cannot be done. Either I don't know how or am unwilling to do it. It is impossible that he doesn't understand the system. "Are you sure? Why don't you just try it. If you are not sure how, you can call one of the other stores and ask someone there how."

By now I had lost all patience. "I am very sure. I don't need to call anyone, and I am not going to try something that I know will not work. I know it won't work because if you look in the manuals about how to put an item on file, it says at the end P.S.: you cannot put beer items on file due to ATF rules! Should I show you where it is in the manual, so you can see it for yourself?"

"You don't need to be disrespectful to me! I came back here and asked you to do this because it's part of your job. The next time I come to you, I expect you not to give me an attitude."

He was about to see just how much attitude I could give. "You came to me because I am the only person in this store who knows how to put items on file properly. You didn't ask me, you told me to do it and then argued with me when I said I could not. You refused to believe me when I tried to tell you about the restrictions in the system. Instead you treated me like I am stupid and don't know my job. I know my job and this computer system very well. Just because you want something done does not always mean that the system will allow it."

We glared at each other a moment, then he looked away. As much as his ego hated to admit it, he had lost this fight. I knew I had made him mad but didn't care about his feelings. I had been through that same scenario with many managers over the years. Most didn't believe me when I said I couldn't help them, but since they had no idea how to do the task themselves and had no idea where to find the instructions, their only option would be to ask someone higher up and risk looking stupid if they were wrong and I was right. And to most managers, there is nothing worse than looking stupid. He stomped off, and I was sure the next employee he met would get the wrath he couldn't give me. Like I said, he needed me.

22

After all my years, I consider myself a retail expert. Not too much comes up that I have not dealt with, even less that I cannot handle. I have honed my problem-solving skills by making mistakes and having to fix them. I have no patience for those who mess up and then throw their hands in the air and cry "my bad" and leave the problem for others to correct. I encounter this almost daily. Any who do this hate to come to me with their mistake because they know the solution will come with some sharp words about paying attention to your job and learning how to do it correctly.

But I know my days are numbered. Major changes to two key positions have happened since this store opened. One job was removed completely; the other was completely changed and most of the employees left the area. Both areas were usually run by long-term employees, and long-term employees are expensive to keep on the payroll. We make more and get way more benefits than those under five years. The only area left in the company that is run almost exclusively by long-term people is mine. And changes have started in my area now.

Not that I mind change. I think I have learned how to roll with changes pretty well by now. Changes are going to happen whether I want them to or not, so there is really no use in fighting them. Of course, not all changes are for the better. In fact, more and more seem to be for the worse. The main problem is that new programs are implemented too soon. Not enough time has been spent at home office working the bugs out. So we try to get the program going, but it quickly falls apart. Then the employees are blamed for the failure (because we didn't run the program properly; never mind all the fact it wouldn't work in the most perfect store). Home office stops the program till further notice. Then a good six months later, it is reintroduced to the stores as an entirely new program. What they have actually done is change about 50 percent of it, fix or remove the bits that didn't work, and try to slide it by us like we will never figure it out.

The changes that have been made to the claims job may sound good on paper but are just making a mess. Until now, the only people who process claims are those of us who work there. It's usually treated like a black hole; everyone leaves broken or leaking items at our door and then acts like the mess doesn't exist. Basically, we are the maids for the store; just leave it for us, and we get to take care of it. This is why anyone who works in claims is usually cranky. You clean up your workspace, and the next day, some jerk has left broken glass all over and maybe some raw chicken leaking on things and a quart of motor oil in a puddle on the floor. If you walked into that kind of mess every day, you would be cranky too. Obviously, that is not what employees are supposed to do, but when the whole management team leaves broken items as they walk by, it's not a shock when the general attitude is to dump and run.

The claims job till now has basically been to take care of all the broken or damaged items in the store properly. My job as the supervisor is to make sure this is happening and verify it is all done correctly and meeting compliance standards by auditing the items we process. The new program took at least half our job away. Supervisors over each area of the sales floor were supposed to come back and process their own items to be disposed or donated, anything else was still our job. Plus, the items being disposed of or donated were done differently, and I could no longer audit them. The supervisors who had processed them were to do the audits themselves. Of course, no one knew how to process any-thing, and we had to show them all what to do. Some eventually learned it, some did not.

It became clear to me on day two that this was going to be a giant mess. I found items in a box marked *dispose* that did not seem to have been processed and other items that showed on the screen as processed but were not in the box. As soon as I found out I could not do any audits on these items, I told management that I washed my hands of it. Since it was no longer my responsibility to process these items and I wasn't able to do the audits and fix any mistakes, this was clearly not my problem. Dirk decided that there wasn't any problem and just ignored the whole situation.

I knew this was not going to be good when it came time for the store's yearly inventory, but since no one else seemed to care, I decided I didn't need to either. Lani had a lot of trouble with this; she was not raised to half-ass her job and not care about the result. I wasn't raised that way either but had been around plenty long enough to learn it is not worth stressing over. I will always do whatever job I have to the best of my abilities, but in the end, it is just a job, and it's not worth raising your blood pressure.

There have been plenty of times over my years when I have been so stressed and frustrated that I was in tears over my job. I've had manage-ment tell me not to be so upset and don't let things get to me. My an-swer back is this: you should be glad that I'm this upset because it means I give a damn about my job. I'm upset because I care. I'm upset because I want to do well, make my area the best it can be, and make the store profitable for us all. If no one is ever frustrated or angry about things go-ing wrong, your workplace may be quiet and calm, but I'll bet produc-tivity is at an all-time low.

I said earlier that Dirk doesn't seem to care how the store runs. The other side is that when you don't care, you don't value your store either. He certainly has not shown that he values any of us, and when employ-ees are not valued, they will never give 100 percent. Indeed, productivity was reaching new lows, along with morale. His favorites strutted around without a care in the world, feeling like they were protected and didn't need to work. Everyone else was disgusted by them and felt no need to do the work of another plus their own. Most stopped doing their own work or did the bare minimum.

The second new program for the store was to change the management structure. Three salaried managers were transferred out, and instead of an hourly supervisor over each area, now there would be zones of many areas together with an hourly supervisor over the zone but doing many jobs of a salaried manager. So, many area supervisors lost their positions; some were promoted to run a zone, and some were demoted or transferred out. The process of choosing who would be promoted turned into a drama fest. Of course, the favorites went around declaring that they would all be promoted. Others who felt they were more qualified got mad, gossip blew through the store like a tornado, and angry phone calls were made to home office, charging Dirk with discrimination. It took two months before final decisions were made and officially announced. He might as well have not bothered at that point, as everyone already knew who had gotten which zone. Of course, for those two months, all work in each area pretty much stopped. Any who were not getting promoted just checked out and said *who cares*. Those who were getting promoted were now looking toward their new areas and didn't care what kind of mess they left for the next person to inherit.

The smooth-running store that Bubba had left was now completely off the tracks. Once the supervisors were running their new zones, they also had to help the managers with store calls and customer issues. Many who had thought that one area was too much work soon realized that many areas in a zone plus new responsibilities was way too much to handle. Within a month, half wanted to step down and give up their new position, but the drama fest had caused us to lose five good area supervisors to another store in town, so now Dirk had no one to replace them. He spent the next month shuffling supervisors around to different zones (as if that was going to make any difference in their attitudes or capabilities), demoting those who insisted on it and promoting anyone willing to give it a try.

By the time our yearly inventory came around, we were not just off the tracks but upside down in a ditch on fire. By now, even his favorites were over it, sick of getting yelled at for the work not getting done. I knew inventory was going to be a mess. I had seen it coming months before. Home office had changed the process this year, but it actually turned out easier to prepare from years before. We all still worked overtime getting ready, but only about half as much as last year. The big day went pretty smoothly too, but as I predicted, we did worse than last year. On the day after, Dirk called us all together to talk about how we did. As he gave the numbers, I gave Lani a knowing look. We both expected the outcome. He then went on to tell us all how he was so glad it was over; he had been working so many extra days and hours that he was just exhausted. As a whole group, we rolled our eyes and said nothing. I guess he got the point because he then thanked all of us for our extra hours and hard work, noting that it was a team effort.

While he tried to save face, our new HR woman decided that she needed to add her two cents. She had been a cashier but got the HR position when that shake-up happened. Most of the long-term HR people didn't like the new job duties and decided to take the retirement payout offered. That left a huge shortage of employees to take the positions, so pretty much anyone who applied got a spot. She was still reveling in her new position of importance and obviously felt the need to share some thoughts anytime three or more employees were around. She piped up and first wanted us to give Dirk a round of applause for all his hard work leading us through inventory. We all glared at her while he got the most pathetic applause ever heard. Silence would have been less embarrassing for him. She went on, undaunted, saying how she thought this new system this year was great. She felt it was a much more accurate inventory than in years past. Lani and I looked at each other and tried not to laugh. Clearly, she did not understand that we had done worse than last year, and her remarks were not a compliment. The look on Dirk's face was priceless. He desperately wanted to shut her up but could not be rude to his one big supporter. When she stopped for a breath, he quickly ended the meeting and sent everyone back to work. Lani and I walked away, laughing and shaking our heads over the whole thing.

A few months into the year, I had been to see my foot doctor. I had my right foot operated on two years before, and now the left foot was really hurting. I tried cortisone shots first; I had two in a month's time. But they didn't help. I had waited too long and now would have to have surgery. I talked with Lani and Jingles; they would be the ones who had to carry on without me. Lani did not want to do inventory without me, especially when we heard about the new system. So, I planned to wait till that was done, but Jingles was getting married in the fall and would be gone over a week. We would both be gone and leave Lani alone during that time. But if I waited till Jingles got married and came back, I would miss most of the holiday season. Lani decided she'd rather work a week alone than have me gone for Black Friday and the holidays. So, I saw the doctor again and set up to have my surgery a week after the inventory. I'd be out for eight weeks, recuperating and resting and letting my foot heal properly before I get back on it forty hours a week.

23

That's where I am now, off work and enjoying every minute of it. It's given me a lot of time to think back about all the years I have spent in retail. When I started writing this, I felt kind of depressed, thinking about poor choices, misspent opportunities, and mostly wasted time. But as I reflect on it, I don't think it's been a waste after all. I've grown as a person and learned so much, not just about the job but about myself. I know what I am capable of, and I am capable of a lot. I have learned I can face trials and tough times and know I will get through them and be tougher for it. I know my strengths and my weaknesses, what I do well and what I can improve. I can keep high standards for myself and my coworkers but still take a few minutes to joke and share a laugh. I don't shy away or hide from problems or mistakes; I know they will come, no matter what, and the best thing is to admit when you are wrong and fix it quickly. Most will say they survived their years in retail, but only a few can say that they thrived.

Now I think about how soon I will leave it forever. One more year, and I will be able to leave it behind and take some little minimum-wage job answering a phone somewhere off my feet for good. One more year of frustration and aggravation, joking and teasing, laughing and swearing and laughing some more. Good friends make bad work easier, and the bonds you form will last long after the work is done. I treasure the friends I made through the long shifts and crappy days, going to hell and back again. They are the truest and most loyal friends I could ever ask for.

Soon I'll be back to work, dealing with the drama with Lani and Jingles. The girls have been keeping me up to date on all the craziness going on. We will get through it together; of that I have no doubt. Lani texted me the other day and just said: "This place sucks without you."

It was the best compliment I have ever received at work.

CHAPTER 24

Epilogue

It's been six months since I came back from my foot surgery. Unfortunately, it has not been a good six months. Stress levels throughout the store are at an all-time high. While I was out, a rift happened between Lani and Jingles. They hardly speak, and I get to play referee between them. Dirk has somehow gotten even more useless. I have never worked with a manager so immature and unprofessional. After a negative review by home office, he no longer hides in his office all day but wanders the store, constantly barking orders into his radio and complaining about everything. No matter what you have done, it is wrong. At least he still leaves me alone, never saying more than hello as he breezes by. That's fine with me; anything I have to say, he does not want to hear. My patience is running very thin; my manager keeps fussing with me about being nicer and watching how I speak to others. Usually I try not to speak so I will stay out of trouble. But sometimes, something just has to be said.

Besides all the normal stress, the pandemic has brought us "essential workers" to our knees. We are just trying to do our jobs and get products on the shelves. Believe me, we certainly are never treated like we are essential, not by management or customers. No matter what is happening at home or how we are feeling we are expected to show up for work. And, expected to keep a civil tongue while being screamed at because of our lack of product on the shelves. The last thing we need to deal with is the whole town breaking down our doors just to add to their collection of toilet paper. In an effort to keep my sanity I wrote this poem about it.

ASSAULT ON AISLE NINETEEN

I'm not sure how it started
Things were going along
In their normal, chaotic way
In the large retail store.
Suddenly there was a tsunami
Of people flooding the aisles
Pushing and shoving
Frantic to grab
As many packages
Of toilet paper as they could
We watched
My coworkers and I
In disbelief as the shelves were picked clean
By the frenzied piranhas
What was happening?
Why did people buy all the toilet paper and leave?
The next day
It happened again
The aisle, restocked and full
Stripped bare
but now the swarm also loaded carts with hand sanitizer
Again, we asked each other

What the hell is going on?
Each day the stampeding herd returned
And each day another item was added to their carts
Toilet paper, hand sanitizer, bottled water, cleaning wipes,
disinfectant sprays
As desperation set in
Paper towels, facial tissue, baby wipes, corn husks
Then someone finally realized they might need to eat
Ramen noodles, pop tarts, pancake mix, cereal, milk, eggs
The bread aisle was decimated
Even the low carb options were gone
All we could say, hiding in the backroom
This is crazy, this is crazy
Each day the ravenous pack grew in size and anger
Why are the shelves empty? Where is everything??
Why don't you have any toilet paper???
They would scream at us
Accusing us of hiding it in the backroom for ourselves
Demanding to know when the truck would deliver more
They camped outside and watched
Waiting to pounce the moment the truck rolled in
Bouncers had to be stationed to block aisles
Just so we could put what little had come
On the shelves and then run for our lives
The aisle was picked bare in mere minutes
And the cycle started again
Each day the news
Cried of disease and pestilence
Quarantine orders
Isolate yourself
Don't go out
But only for essentials
Which to the American consumer
Meant everything

Puzzle books, batteries, insoles, feta cheese, pork rinds,
kitchen towels
Don't forget to check the clearance aisle, there might be some
good deals on car seat covers and fishing lures
The panic continued to spread
Now the horde bought dog food and kitty litter
It might save them as a last resort
Should their garage full of corn flakes and 3000 rolls of
toilet paper run out
We huddled in the backroom, terrified
Drew lots to see who would have to risk their life
Restocking the canned peaches
Was the whole world mad?
We begged for it to end, lighting candles, chanting supplications
We had nothing to offer the retail gods in exchange for mercy
All food and supplies were taken by the uncontrolled mob
Might as well search for a unicorn than a virgin
What could we do but try to encourage each other
Draw strength from those who faced the
raging customers and survived
Those of us
The old guard
Who had fought through many Black Fridays
Told stories of brave deeds, mighty acts of courage
The good old days
Where it was only for one night
Then it passed
But this, this continued
Day after day
No end in sight
Two weeks
Thirty days
Six weeks
Or more

The projections grew more depressing
Our spirits, already bruised and beaten
Now crushed, decimated
We look to the manager
For guidance, wisdom, just one encouraging word
But he took the week off
He had new carpet installed at his house
Left to fend for ourselves
We picked up weapons
Armed ourselves
Prepared to protect our brother
As he builds a towering display
Of two hundred cases of creamed corn
Wish us luck in our quest
May we all come back alive

After so many years I've reached the end of my capacity to keep showing up and working hard for no acknowledgment or appreciation. I'm over it, and it is time to go. I just passed my anniversary milestone of thirty years. I told management that I didn't want any fuss, and I meant it. If I'm not valued the rest of the year, I don't need them to pretend they value me for one day. It makes me a bit sad to see how things are ending, but I guess it is not that different from the beginning, when my first manager told me she would fire me in a week. Not quite "a thousand years as a day." Instead, thirty years as a week. But it's been a very long week, and I sure am ready for the weekend. Maybe I will treat myself to a three-day weekend. I think I have earned it.

P.S.: Right after I wrote this epilogue, I started applying places for a new job. My timing was good, and I had five interviews in ten days. I accepted a job with the state and put in my notice. I am very excited for my new position, where I will be off my feet and working in an air-conditioned office. And I didn't feel one bit sorry that my I started my new job just one day before the store's yearly inventory!